Building *Positive* Relationships

Freeing our present from our past

Len Kofler MHM

Director of the Institute of St Anselm, Kent

redemptorist
publications

Published by Redemptorist Publications
Alphonsus House, Chawton, Hampshire, GU34 3HQ, UK
Tel. +44 (0)1420 88222, Fax. +44 (0)1420 88805
Email rp@rpbooks.co.uk, www.rpbooks.co.uk

A registered charity limited by guarantee
Registered in England 3261721

Copyright © Len Kofler 2015
First published May 2015

Edited by Denis McBride and Therese Garman
Designed by Peena Lad

ISBN 978-0-85231-426-5

A CIP catalogue record for this book is available from the British Library.

The publisher gratefully acknowledges permission to use the following copyright material:

Excerpts from *The Jerusalem Bible*, copyright © 1966 by Darton, Longman & Todd, Ltd
and Doubleday, a division of Random House, Inc. Reprinted by permission.

Printed by Bishops Printers Limited, Portsmouth PO6 1TR

Acknowledgments

My reflections on relationships have been informed by students and friends, too numerous to mention, in the Missionary Institute, London, and the Institute of St Anselm. I am most grateful to all participants who followed courses over thirty years and staff with whom I worked during this time. They all enriched my understanding of relationships which had already been expanded through working in Ireland, Austria, New Zealand, Italy and the United Kingdom.

The foundations for my personal relationships were laid in my family with my dear parents, brothers and sisters to whom I am deeply grateful, in a lively parish and village atmosphere. Later the international St Joseph's Missionary Society, with its multicultural background, widened the horizon of relationships. The Maori people with their extraordinary emphasis on community living, among whom I worked for over five years and enjoyed speaking their language, gave me many new insights into human relationships in a different culture.

I am most grateful to Redemptorist Publications for accepting my manuscript, especially Denis McBride, the Publications Director, who encouraged me to write. Therese Garman as a skilled and thorough editor deserves special thanks. Thalia was always willing to be a sounding board and to help me with my computer when I got stuck. John McCluskey gave me many valuable suggestions and Claire McGuire was always there with her moral support. To all of you I would like to express my sincere gratitude.

I pray for each reader of this book that it may enrich their relationships and bring deep peace and joy into their lives.

Len Kofler

By the same author

Healing Relationships: A practical guide for Christian counsellors and carers

Healing Groups: A practical guide for Christian leaders

Looking After Yourself: A Christian guide to a balanced life

Leadership and Formation: The story of the development of the Catholic Institute for Leadership and Formation

"Pope Francis' Journey: A journey for all of us" in *The Francis Factor* edited by John Littleton & Eamon Maher

Contents

Chapter three The importance of trust in relationships

Chapter four The importance of good communication in relationships

Chapter five The important role emotions play in relationships

Preface

For the past thirty years, Fr Len Kofler has directed the Institute of St Anselm in Cliftonville, Kent, which he founded in 1985. This remarkable educational and spiritual power-house has served as an incomparable resource for countless priests, religious and lay people who are in significant leadership roles in the Church or who are preparing for such responsibilities. The Institute has drawn its students from many nationalities and cultures. For three decades it has seen the emergence of international communities characterised by a spirit of deep respectfulness and by a prizing of each member in all his or her uniqueness. It is rare for one man's vision to be so vividly realised as is the case with the history of the Institute of St Anselm.

Fr Len is inspired by the conviction that human beings are reflections of the divine nature and are consequently most wonderfully made and of infinite complexity. Each of us owes it to ourselves and to our fellow members of the human family to extend the breadth of our self-awareness. We can then become increasingly integrated and guard against the fragmentation which our current cultures so often exacerbate.

For Fr. Len it makes no sense to think of spiritual development without, at the same time, paying equal attention to emotional and intellectual growth. So often, it seems, persons in leadership roles – and the Church is no exception – fail in their tasks because of an inability to relate effectively to colleagues and others in their care. Sometimes they also lack the emotional and intellectual maturity necessary for leading groups and communities.

Those who study and train at the Institute of St Anselm undergo a rigorous apprenticeship which demands an investment of the whole person and does not evade the struggle and the pain which are inevitably involved as blocks to growth are exposed, past hurts are revealed and negative patterns of behaviour are confronted. The spiritual journey is no undertaking for the faint-hearted and requires emotional courage.

Fr Len's new book is in many ways a distillation of a lifetime's experience as priest, trainer, therapist and spiritual accompanist. Above all, it offers the quintessential wisdom of someone who throughout a long life has yearned to be a fully-functioning human being, someone who has resolutely turned his back on a spurious spirituality which colludes with an evasion of self-knowledge and induces a fear of intimacy. Readers of *Building Positive Relationships* are gently led into terrain which may at first seem frightening. With Fr Len as one's guide, however, the fear of the unknown and the facing of pain from the past gradually give way to the exhilaration of a new-found liberty which comes from self-acceptance.

This is a challenging book but it is ultimately a hopeful one. It asks for commitment to the sometimes arduous task of becoming the kind of human being who knows how to love and how to receive love. It also invites us to face the astonishing truth that we are loved by a God whose love is almost unbearable in its intensity.

Brian Thorne
Emeritus Professor of Counselling, University of East Anglia
Co-founder, the Norwich Centre for Personal, Professional and Spiritual Development
Lay Canon, Norwich Cathedral.

How to Use this Book

Books can be used in many ways depending on what you would like to gain from them. Some people read a book quickly to have an overall view; others go through it more reflectively looking for personal enrichment. This book may be used in many ways; the pictures may invite you to meditate. You can read and work with the chapters in any order.

My recommendation is to use this book as a journey towards inner freedom. There is a difference between reading a book for insight and reading a book for personal development. This latter requires reflection and is facilitated through the questions in each chapter. The insights you gain invite you to practise on a daily basis. For example, if you become aware that often you don't listen to other people, you may practise this skill when you have the opportunity.

Give yourself ten to fifteen minutes each day to do the reflective exercises. Once you have gained insight into your behaviour and wish to change it, you can apply the insights to yourself and your relationships. Be patient: habits change slowly. It took many years to acquire them, it will take time to change them. Be patient with yourself and you will learn to be patient with others.

Have a notebook and pen to hand to write down your thoughts and discoveries after reflecting on the questions. (It will become a personal 'book of revelation'.) That evening or the next day, write in the notebook how you feel about what you have achieved. Don't be disappointed if you did not succeed. Keep on practising. Be optimistic and foster positive beliefs that you will succeed in this exciting journey of self-discovery.

This book is a companion for the rest of your life. You are encouraged to go over it again and again and you will discover new things about yourself every time. Never forget the Greek saying of the importance of 'knowing yourself' as a way to wisdom.

You can also give a present of this book to a friend and invite them to enter this journey of discovery. Both of you can share part of this journey and support each other on the way.

This companion is meant to accompany you throughout your life on your journey towards inner freedom and peace. As you work daily on yourself, gaining many insights and putting them into practice, your whole life becomes more and more exciting and meaningful. You are discovering new territories in yourself. It is like a journey into your alienated and unknown self, which will empower you to take responsibility for your life.

Len Kofler

Chapter one

Introduction: Freeing our present from our past – a key to our relationships

The importance of relationships

We can hardly exaggerate the importance of relationships in our lives. We have relationships with people, animals, things, the environment, suffering and God. We learned to relate to all of these in early childhood. But not all of our relationships are healthy; some may even be destructive.

The human heart has a deep desire for healthy relationships. There is nothing more beautiful than to see such a desire fulfilled in people. Obviously, perfect relationships exist only in the community of the Blessed Trinity. However, each one of us can work to improve our relationships. It is more valuable to spend time on this than on many other activities. The reward is a high degree of happiness and a deep sense of fulfilment.

Difficulties in relationships

Sometimes we may wonder why we lose friends. We may ask ourselves: "Why can't I get on with people? I've tried so hard." If you are one of those people who wish to make efforts to improve your relationships, this book will help you in your endeavours.

Blaming others for the difficulties

Frequently people think that it is the fault of the other person that they can't get on with them, so they look for another relationship. Soon they find out that the new relationship does not work either. Their conviction is that again the other person is at fault and so they have to find yet another relationship. They are blind to the fact that something in their own lives might need to change.

My part in relationship problems

When problems arise in relationships, we need to own that we are part of the problem. As long as we deny this and blame others for it, we cannot move forward. We need to become aware of how we are part of the difficulties. Often when people have problems in their relationships, they are unaware that the underlying cause is to be found earlier in their life. Our past interferes with our present. You might say: "How can the past interfere with the present? It's gone; it's not in the here-and-now". Yes, the time is gone, but not the effects of our past experiences. They are still with us – helping us or hindering us.

Our past interferes with our present

What we learned in the past will influence our present behaviour. Not all that we learned as children is helpful for us as adults. We may need to unlearn many things which we learned as children. This is definitely my experience. And yet I am still most grateful to my parents and siblings for the positive things I acquired in my family. They are many. Not everybody may have had good experiences when they were children. However, healthy relationships in the here-and-now will heal the wounds of the destructive relationships in earlier life. Nobody needs to despair.

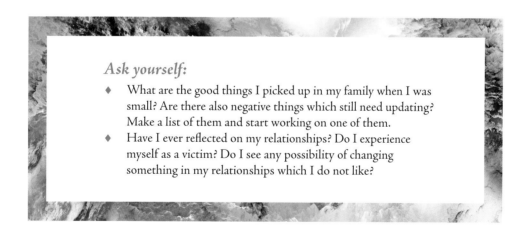

Ask yourself:

♦ What are the good things I picked up in my family when I was small? Are there also negative things which still need updating? Make a list of them and start working on one of them.

♦ Have I ever reflected on my relationships? Do I experience myself as a victim? Do I see any possibility of changing something in my relationships which I do not like?

Illustration of the fear of dogs

When I was three years old, I went with my brother, who was four years older than I, into a forest. We passed a house with a small garden, where there was a dog running up and down barking at us. My brother said to me: "Be careful, dogs bite you." Only relatively recently did I get rid of my fear of dogs. I had learned that dogs bite, so I was afraid of them, particularly if they opened their mouth or barked. I avoided them as much as I could and never learned to relate to them. When I went for a walk and saw a dog coming, I turned round and went in the opposite direction. I had generalised the words of my brother and thought that all dogs were biters.

Fifteen years ago, my friend bought a dog. I was afraid of him, but could not avoid being with her and the dog in the same house – we were working in an educational institute and lived on the premises. It was extremely painful for me. Many times when the dog barked, it went like an electric shock through my body. We went to see her mother who also had a dog. I watched the two dogs playing with each other with open mouths. I observed that in spite of that they were very gentle with each other, jaws open but not biting. This was an enormous learning point for me, unlearning what I had learned as a child. Slowly I felt less anxious in the presence of my friend's dog.

About a month later, my friend said to me: "You can touch the dog, he won't bite you." I started by touching him near the tail, and then slowly I dared to move my hands closer to his head. As I gradually got rid of my fear, I began to enjoy him and even to play with him. I established a very friendly relationship with him and after a year I had learned to distinguish between a dangerous dog and a friendly dog.

What brought about this change in me? I learned to 'relate' to dogs. Before that, I avoided them and therefore had no relationship with them. Relating to dogs helped me to get rid of my fear and to start enjoying them.

My past had dominated my present for many years, because I had avoided any encounter with dogs. I feel so free now that I can enjoy, rather than avoid, them. By relating to them, not only did I overcome the fear but now I truly love them. Fear casts out love and love casts out fear.

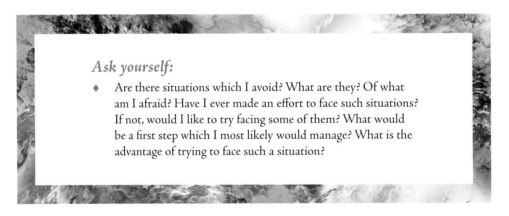

Ask yourself:

♦ Are there situations which I avoid? What are they? Of what am I afraid? Have I ever made an effort to face such situations? If not, would I like to try facing some of them? What would be a first step which I most likely would manage? What is the advantage of trying to face such a situation?

The same is true with regard to people. We may have learned to be afraid of certain people – authority figures, for example. Or we may be afraid of men or of women. We can ask ourselves: "When did I learn this fear? How have I managed to maintain it? Do I want to get rid of this fear? What can I do to rid myself of it?"

Very early in our lives, we learn to relate to people, to animals, to things, to the environment and also to God. As we grow up we unlearn certain things and begin to relate differently. However, this does not happen in all areas of our lives. Even as adults we may still relate to God in the same way as we learned to relate to Him in childhood. This may be the reason why some people give up their belief in God.

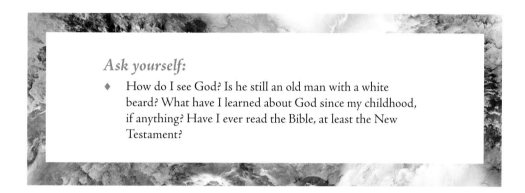

Ask yourself:

♦ How do I see God? Is he still an old man with a white beard? What have I learned about God since my childhood, if anything? Have I ever read the Bible, at least the New Testament?

Illustration of the fear of heights

When I was eight years old, I was looking after the cows in a forest near a high mountain. One of my older brothers came in the afternoon to see how I was getting on with my job. I had looked up at the mountain and saw half way up a green patch of land. I said to my brother: "Let's climb the mountain; it won't take us long." He told me that there was a path on the other side of the valley which led up to that inviting patch of land. But I insisted that it was shorter to climb the mountain from where we were.

The first part of the climb was very easy; we had no problems. Then we went too far to the right of the mountain near a waterfall, because we had no overview of the mountain. What had looked to be an easy climb became more and more difficult, until we reached an overhanging rock which we had to master, since there was no other way forward. I looked down; it looked like thousands of feet. We knew we could not go back, because that was too dangerous. I cried and prayed, afraid to look into the devouring depths below.

After many efforts my brother, who was much taller than I, managed to reach and grip on to the overhanging rock and said to me: "I'll pull you up, you just hold on to my hand; I'll hold on to the rock with my other hand." After some hesitation, I entrusted myself to the strength of his hand to pull me up hanging in the air. I was terrified to look down into the depths below. Miraculously, we managed to overcome this frightening obstacle of the overhanging rock and then safely reached the top of the mountain. We were both exhausted and lay down in the grass.

From this terrifying experience I acquired a fear of heights. I was afraid even to use ropes to climb mountains. Although many of my friends have climbed the Grossglockner, the highest mountain in Austria, I never dared to join them. I am still afraid of heights. We can never heal all areas of our lives which were damaged by earlier experiences. However, there are many aspects which do need changing so that our present lives can become better. The fact that I am still afraid of heights doesn't worry me because it does not affect my daily life. I do not intend to climb high mountains, since I have had open heart surgery. But I am very pleased that I am no longer afraid of dogs because I encounter them on my daily walks, an essential part of my healthy living.

These two examples show us how our relationship with the environment is influenced by past experiences. Past events have shaped our present relationships in many ways. Some experiences were responsible for our present healthy relationships; others for our hurtful and negative ones. Getting to know our past history will help us to understand our present behaviours, motivations, emotions, values and many other aspects of our lives.

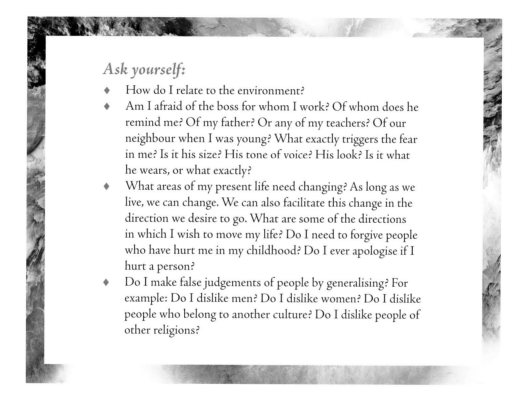

Ask yourself:

- ♦ How do I relate to the environment?
- ♦ Am I afraid of the boss for whom I work? Of whom does he remind me? Of my father? Or any of my teachers? Of our neighbour when I was young? What exactly triggers the fear in me? Is it his size? His tone of voice? His look? Is it what he wears, or what exactly?
- ♦ What areas of my present life need changing? As long as we live, we can change. We can also facilitate this change in the direction we desire to go. What are some of the directions in which I wish to move my life? Do I need to forgive people who have hurt me in my childhood? Do I ever apologise if I hurt a person?
- ♦ Do I make false judgements of people by generalising? For example: Do I dislike men? Do I dislike women? Do I dislike people who belong to another culture? Do I dislike people of other religions?

Desire for perfect relationships: The Blessed Trinity as our model

I have read novels and looked at films trying to find model relationships. Though I may admire some character in a novel, I always detect imperfections in him or her. I suppose I want a perfect model of relationships for my life. In my search over many years I have now found such a model. It is the person of Christ. I am particularly fascinated by what Jesus says about His Father in heaven and the Holy Spirit. Their relationships fascinate me and have become a model for my own relationships. I am constantly inspired by the way they are with each other, beautifully expressed in Rublev's icon. For me it expresses in an artistic way the relationships of the Blessed Trinity. I also love to read St John's Gospel. Thus I find plenty of food to nourish my spirituality and my curiosity about relationships.

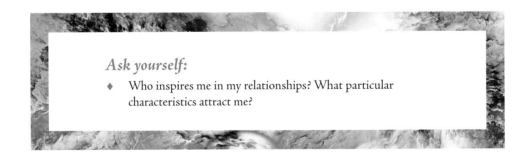

Ask yourself:

♦ Who inspires me in my relationships? What particular characteristics attract me?

Christ's life and teaching has shaped my life in many ways, especially in my attitude to suffering. As a child I learned that Christ suffered for us and redeemed us through his suffering and death on the cross, because he loved us so much. I no longer see suffering just as an evil to be avoided at any cost. I see it now as a means of healing and growing. How many people have matured through very painful experiences in their lives? Three years ago I had open heart surgery. My relationship to suffering, picked up in childhood, helped me to have hope and find meaning in this situation, and actually to enjoy my stay in hospital, where I received excellent care and treatment. How I related to suffering was key to my recovery.

I have mentioned four different relationships: the relationship to dogs, to heights, to Christ and to suffering. The focus in this book is on human relationships. I just wanted to illustrate the importance of all kinds of relationships in our lives, how we learned these relationships and how we can unlearn them, if we wish.

Relationships are extremely important in our lives. They can have a healing effect or they can destroy us. They can build us up or tear us down. It is well worthwhile reflecting on our own relationships to find out what they do to us. However, we must never forget our part in the relationship. We have choices. We contribute to the relationship. Sometimes, it looks as if something just happens to us, as if we have no part in it. Sometimes we may react to a situation in a way that surprises us. Even in these situations, we can do something about it, as we shall see later on in this book.

To do:

♦ When we look at our lives, it is important not to forget the positive aspects of our past history. There are so many factors which have influenced our lives. Even some negative elements may not bother us now too much, because they are not so relevant for our present functioning. Write a short autobiography of what influenced you in becoming the person you are now.

Ask yourself:

♦ What relationships do I want to improve as I read this book?
♦ What do I want to get out of this book? What must I do to achieve this goal?
   [Reading this book is not enough, we need to practise what we read, not just as an exercise, but in our daily life.]
♦ Relationships are central to our lives. It takes time to unlearn what we have learned and acquire new habits. Am I willing to invest time and energy into improving my relationships, in making sure they are fruitful, healthy and positive? What would my future be like if I did this?
♦ Just imagine what life would be like, if I did take ten minutes a day to read this book and try to apply the contents to myself.

Conclusions

As we have seen in this chapter, we can remedy and heal wounds inflicted in our childhood. We do not need to stay in the victim role. We can transform many negative experiences of our past life, which affect our relationships in the here-and-now, into positive outcomes. We are no longer helpless in any of our relationships, provided we are willing to work through the negative or one-sided learning of the past. The working through is illustrated in the relationship with dogs. It takes small steps of learning and unlearning, of observing and relating to the feared person, animal or thing. We can move from fear to love.

Chapter two

*Love is the basis of
healthy relationships*

What true love is not

Love is one of those words which have different meanings for different people. It is essential that we get a clear understanding of what love is. Some think, for example, that people who really love each other never hurt each other. So they never forgive the pain inflicted upon them by a spouse or close friend, because their expectations were not met.

Other people identify love with sex: if a girl really loves a boy, she must show it by having sex with him. He pays for the dinner, but she is then expected to fulfil his sexual desires. He wants to use her for his own gratification and is surprised if she refuses his demand.

Some parents will send their children to an expensive boarding school to make sure that they get the best education. They are surprised to hear from them later that they thought their parents did not love them, because they sent them away.

There are parents who see how some other people's children grow up without being taught any discipline and they do not want their children to grow up in the same way. So they decide to have clear rules for them and see to it that they keep them. They punish them when they go against the rules, for example, depriving them from watching TV. Children pick up the message that they are only loved when they do what their parents want them to do. They never manage to link discipline with love in their minds, because of the strong emotions parents have when their children disobey.

There are parents who do everything for their children, even when they are already adults, and feel that this is the love which they should have for them. They are unaware of the negative effects this inappropriate manifestation of love can have on family relationships.

Some would describe love as the warm feeling that you have for a person who meets all your needs. This person may be a compulsive helper and acts out of his or her compulsion. The person helped may have many neurotic needs. Neither of them may grow in this relationship because both are satisfying their unhealthy needs in this process.

There are those who say: "I love you", with the expectation of finding somebody who will love them, too. It is their need for love which makes them say this and it is actually a manipulation. People may feel obliged to say: "I love you, too."

Even when people say that they have fallen in love with a person, it may not be true love. It may have more to do with loneliness which they try to overcome to bring a good feeling into their life. They interpret this warmth as love for the other person. Some people are so in need of love that they are willing to make compromises. They may compromise their values in order to receive "half a measure" of love. They may allow themselves to be abused because of their strong need of love and belonging.

What is true love?

We have seen above what true love is not. It seems easier to say what love is not than to state what true love is, in spite of the fact that there is a deep longing in our souls for the experience of true love. People crave real love and become vulnerable in its pursuit. "Can I trust this person to receive true love? Can I learn to love and how do I do it? Will love last or will it die?" These are some of the questions people ask themselves.

This four-letter word has produced more songs, stories, poems, soap operas, sermons and books than any other word and still very few people know what true love is. It contains the deepest truths about us and God. God is love. It is like a fire that gives out warmth to all people around. Love reaches out to all and has goodwill for all. When we love a person, we want them to become all they long for. Love is a healing presence to a person, without expecting anything in return. You feel that God is there.

Love means to be close to someone, to share our view of life with them, to feel safe enough to be ourselves in their presence. Love gives us deep peace, joy and happiness in the midst of our fears, doubts and struggles. People long for a perfect experience of love. True love is powerful enough to escort imperfect people through the changing stages of their lives together.

Love between two people is usually complicated because we are all different. People will struggle and sometimes feel like giving up and finding somebody else with whom it is easier to get on. However, we take ourselves with us, wherever we go. It is more useful, and healthier, to stop blaming the other person and to see problems as opportunities for personal growth and development. True love is found only in imperfect hearts of struggling people.

People are meant to grow. Growth is uneven, challenging and surprising. People never get things quite right; they make mistakes and fall short of their own expectations and the expectations of others. Yet perfection haunts them still. This can be dehumanizing and defeating. Only God is perfect. Perfection is a divine quality. We are all called to become more perfect, even in the art of loving, although we will never reach perfection.

Fear of love and loving

Once a student came to me and shared his discovery of himself. He said: "I will never establish a deeper loving relationship because the last one was so painful for me when I had to let go of it." I asked him: "What will happen to you, if you do this?" "I will never be hurt again." Because of the fear of getting hurt, he wanted to avoid deeper relationships and the opportunities for further growth. Loving relationships always carry the danger of loss and separation. Love always carries a risk that we might be rejected when we reach out to another person.

We may be afraid of loving a person because we have been betrayed in a loving relationship. It will take time to build up trust again. Intimacy reveals the truth about us. People are often afraid to face the truth which is revealed in open intimacy.

As love matures in us it leads to stability in our relationships. It becomes a solid base on which to stand close to another person in years to come. In spite of the fact that we do not know the storms that will come our way in the future, we have a solid base in our maturing love. Love aims at wholeness and integration. Only true love gives people the strength to go through all the struggles to grow and mature.

How can we learn true love?

Self-love

We need to learn first to love ourselves. We cannot love others without loving ourselves.

"Love your neighbour as yourself" (Mark 12:31). Very often the second part of the sentence is forgotten. In fact many people learn to love their neighbour at the expense of the self.

The way we relate to others depends on the way we relate to ourselves. If we want to improve our relationships with other people, we may need to learn to improve our relationship with ourselves. Frequently people learn to hate themselves. How can they love their neighbour? Hating ourselves is no gift to God, our neighbour or ourselves. It is hurtful to all around us. Hatred destroys, love builds up.

"We are made in the image and likeness of God" (Gen.1:26-28). God is love. So we are loveable. Do I experience myself as loveable? Sometimes? All the time? If not, why not? It has to do with the way we grew up. We may have acquired low self-esteem, so it is important that we improve it. Low self-esteem is a factor in self-defeating behaviour. Self-confidence is the key to success. The underpinning of low self-confidence is low self-esteem. People do not value themselves but see themselves in negative contrast to others. Self-confidence means to value self.

It does little good to know that we have no confidence in self and low self-esteem, it only serves to make us feel worse. A person with low self-worth has developed a lifestyle which has become second nature. It is like a familiar dress. It is not so pretty or comfortable, but it is there. A friend pays us a compliment, but we feel worthless and can't accept it. We have conditioned ourselves to apologise. We feel tight in the body in spite of the compliment.

A person, who has high self-worth genuinely thanks someone if they pay him or her a compliment. He or she recognizes inwardly that it is true.

Why do so many people feel undeserving? They are brought up that way. Normally we get very little training in valuing ourselves. "Be nice to others" usually means at the expense of yourself. You may have heard the message: "Don't think well of yourself because it is selfish." We may have learned to be a doormat.

We can learn to value ourselves. We can learn to have high self-esteem. We can learn to have self-confidence despite past learning. We have to learn how human beings function. We can also acquire the skills to be effective human beings. "Everything has its beauty but not everyone sees it" (Confucius).

Healthy self-esteem is the fertilizer which nourishes our talents, resources, and abilities. The more positive and pervasive the self-esteem, the richer the soil within which we grow. Poor self-esteem is the root cause of many other behavioural and emotional problems such as alcoholism, eating disorders, depression, child abuse, juvenile delinquency and many more.

Counsellors, teachers, social workers, parents, priests and employers need to know more about the way to improve self-esteem. "Love your neighbour as yourself" implies the necessity of having positive regard for ourselves in order to love our neighbour. We see the world through the filter of self. The view of self, colours and influences all of how we think, feel and act. Self is the frame of reference for all perception.

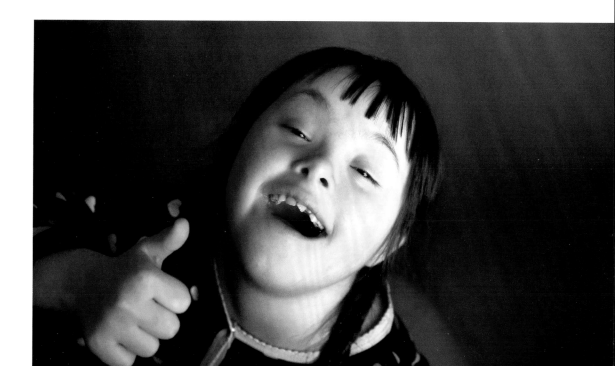

Self-acceptance

Some people struggle to accept certain aspects of their personality. They have been told as children that they are not clever or intelligent, are stupid, useless, hopeless cases, ugly, been compared unfavourably to siblings etc. and have internalised these messages. Now they find it difficult to accept themselves, having generalised these messages. They may feel inadequate, stupid, ugly, not clever, and so on.

Now as adults they have the chance to change this misconception. They can break the hold it has on their life in the here-and-now. They can give themselves different and realistic messages about themselves. By frequently doing that, their behaviour and their feelings will change.

Self-confidence

People benefit from an increase in self-confidence. They feel better about themselves. They will try out new things, discover their talents and seize new opportunities. They can fulfil their potential and discover their purpose in life. People will enjoy being with them. Self-confidence is not the same as arrogance. A self-confident person will admit when they make a mistake. Self-confidence and humility go together. There are areas in our lives where we need to ask others to help us. Humility to ask others for help will increase our self-confidence.

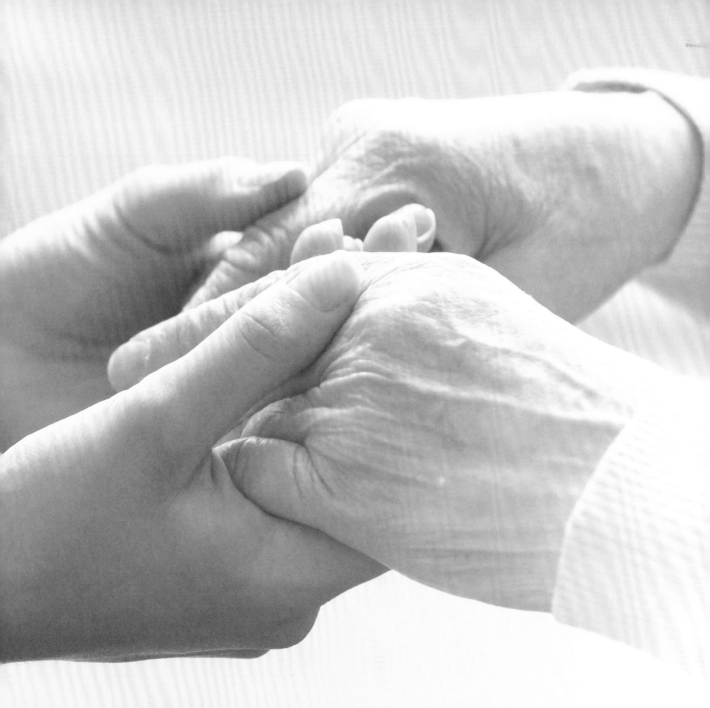

Love is the basis of healthy relationships

How to improve our self-esteem

To improve our self-esteem is not a quick fix. It will take time, but it is time well-spent because it affects our whole being. We are invited to practise not just one exercise, but many. We can do some exercises in front of a mirror and make sure that we smile as we say convincingly: "I am lovable." "I am a responsible person."

Below are various hints and ways as to how you can improve your self-esteem. There is a selection as not all of them may suit you. Among the many you will find some which appeal to you and you can start with those to acquire a healthy self-worth.

♦ Often people with low self-esteem put themselves down if the slightest thing goes wrong. "Why was I so stupid and did not foresee that this would not work out?" Such thoughts come to them. Instead of entertaining these thoughts, they can say to themselves: "What can I learn from this situation?" Thus, any failure situation is turned into a learning experience. If we learn from such experiences, they have had a positive outcome.

- Whenever we become negative in our thoughts about ourselves and become aware of it, we can stop the negativity and search for positive thoughts. This can be difficult at first, because we may be so used to seeing ourselves in such a negative light that it may feel as if the positive thoughts are not true. Still, we need to keep on sending ourselves positive messages which somehow we know are true, even if they do not feel as if they are.

- We can meditate on the command: "Love your neighbour as yourself." God made us in his own image and likeness. He is love, so we too are lovable. God wants us to love ourselves. Frequent meditation on this passage will change our feelings about ourselves over a period of time.

- Learn to choose helpful thoughts about yourself. For example, "I am a considerate and understanding person. People like to come to me."

- Make a point of listening to and respecting your feelings, whatever they are, without acting them out. As you listen to your feelings and become aware of them, try to find out what messages they are sending you. For example, you may be angry because your son was rough with you. Do you feel belittled because of his treatment of you? You can say to yourself: "It has nothing to do with me; it is his behaviour; he is obviously angry". Or "I was nagging him too much. I can learn not to annoy him unnecessarily".

- You may feel hurt. It is important that you do not cling to the hurt and blame the other person. Let go of the blame. Own the feeling of hurt and stay with it for some time. You may get some insights into hurts in the past. You may even discover a whole history about your hurts and understand how they are linked together. You will acquire more self-knowledge and self-understanding.

- I have written a book entitled *Looking after yourself*. We need to learn to look after ourselves. This self-care will help us to feel good about ourselves.

- Let go of grievances. They eat you up. Get on with what is important in your life.

- Don't stay in the victim role. You waste energy. Take responsibility for your life and actions.

- Develop your spiritual life by finding time to meditate, pray and think of the ultimate things and find meaning in them. Never forget that God loves you in spite of all your weaknesses. His love is unconditional.

- Do not compare yourself to others and their performance. You are unique and by comparing yourself to others you do an injustice to yourself. You may have learned to do that in childhood. Now you can change it. Do justice to your own uniqueness.

- Your parents or parent-substitutes may have expected too much of you or too little. Learn now to have realistic expectations of yourself. If your parents expected too much of you and you couldn't live up to their expectations and failed, it may have affected your self-esteem. On the other hand, if they had few expectations of you, you may have learnt that you are not able to do things which you could actually do. Again it affected your self-worth. Now you have the chance to change this. Become aware of your expectations. You may have made your parents' or parent-substitutes' expectations your own. This is your chance now to acquire a healthy self-esteem by having realistic expectations of yourself.

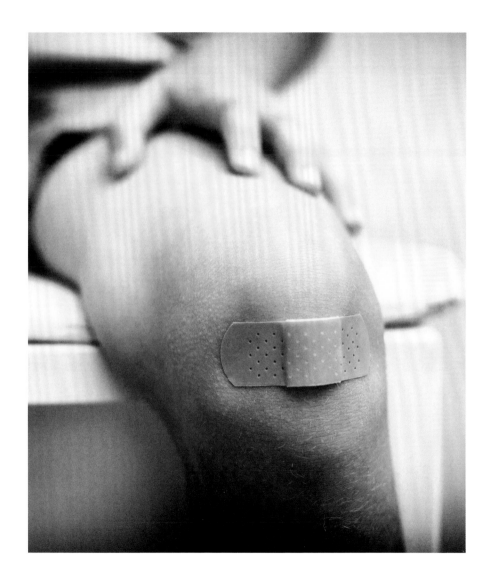

- Keep the love Christ has for you constantly in your mind. You have a friend who will never leave you, who always loves you, who suffered for you and died for you on the cross, who went to his Father in heaven to prepare a place for you. You are so precious to him. These frequent thoughts will enkindle love in you for him. In this warm atmosphere of true love, your self-esteem will grow like a plant grows in the sunshine.

- As your relationship with yourself improves, notice how your relationships with others change. This will encourage you to keep on working on yourself. You may dare to ask a person to go for a walk with you, which you could not have done before. You might have a discussion with a friend and give your own opinion, which you never dared to do before. You might initiate a discussion on a topic which would have been impossible for you to do before. As you become aware of how working on improving your self-concept influences many other areas in your life for the better, you will feel encouraged to keep on with your work of acquiring a healthy self-worth.

- Make frequent efforts to relax your body by deep breathing, especially when you go for walks. Look after your physical health. It will help you to be positive about yourself. When you are not well, accept the situation, do what you can to become better and stop blowing things up out of proportion, if you are in the habit of doing this.

- Even our posture can influence our self-esteem. We can all learn confident posture. Many people have developed a poor self-image posture. Their posture communicates: "I am worthless. I should not exist. Sorry I am here." Developing a confident posture will help to improve our self-esteem.

- We need to learn to use "master" language and not "slave" language. This means that we have to cut out many of our 'shoulds', 'oughts' 'musts' and substitute them with, 'I would like to do it', 'I have chosen to do it' or 'I won't do it', 'I have decided not to do it'. The kind of language we use will affect our self-concept.

- We can learn to live with more awareness. This will help us to confront ourselves, to respect our reality whether it is pleasant or painful, to take appropriate risks, to be honest with ourselves, to be responsible for the present and to see and correct mistakes. All these efforts will improve our self-worth.

- When we have learned to accept ourselves, it does not mean that we have no desire to change, develop and improve. In fact, self-acceptance is the precondition for change. For example, I accept that I feel worthless and I know that I learned to feel worthless in school, but now I want to change this feeling into feeling good about myself.

- Stand in front of a full-length mirror and look at your body. What do you see? What do you not want to see? Become aware of these parts. You may not want to look at certain parts of your body. You may try to avoid looking at them. Just stay focused on what you see for a few moments. As you repeat the same exercise later or next day, stay a few minutes longer with the parts you wish to avoid. You may not like your big nose or big ears. It may remind you of the many times your mother pulled your ears. Looking at your nose may remind you of the many times other children made fun of it. You carry on doing this exercise until you feel comfortable with each part of your body. As you do the exercise, say to yourself: God created me and he loves me the way I am. If God loves me the way I am, I will also learn to love myself the way I am.

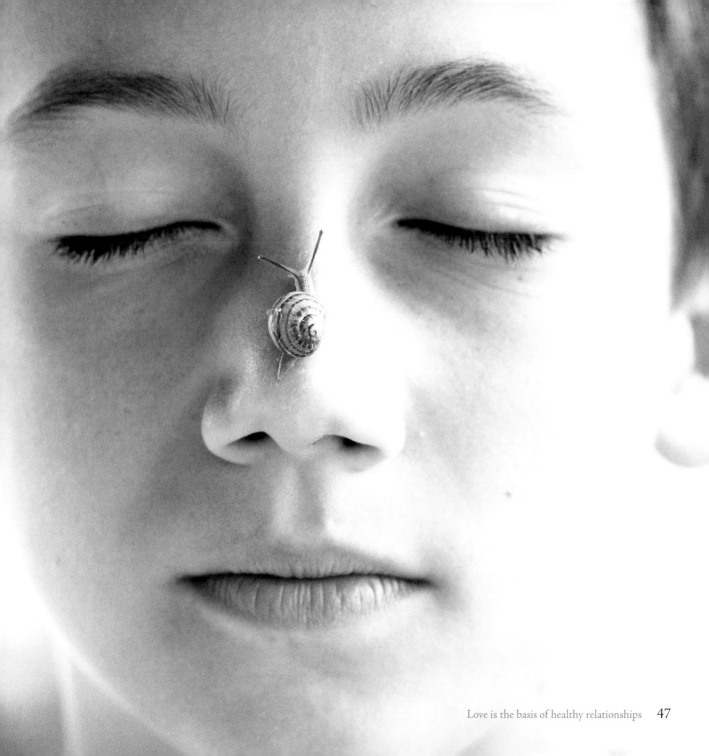

♦ Take time and try to stay with a feeling you find difficult to accept. It could be insecurity, pain, envy, rage, humiliation, fear, jealousy, rejection etc. Try to isolate one feeling and bring it into clear focus. You can think or imagine whatever might evoke it. Breathe deeply into the feeling. Imagine what it would be like and what it would feel like if you could accept the feeling fully. Then say to yourself: "I now accept this feeling fully". This may not be easy at the beginning. Your body may become tense. You need to persevere. Keep on breathing deeply. Allow your muscles to relax. Give the feeling permission to be there. Evoke your curiosity to explore the world of feelings in you by staying with each one of them. This will lead to self-acceptance.

♦ Suppose the feeling we want to focus on is so distressing that we cannot accept it, and therefore we block it and contract. We must not resist our resistance. We need to accept it. We start to accept where we are. We are aware of our resistance and we stay with it. We allow it to be in our conscious mind. After some time the resistance will dissolve. When we acknowledge, experience and accept our resistance, it begins to collapse. When we fight a block, it grows stronger. When we accept it, it begins to melt away.

♦ Life is a constant learning experience without us realising it. Sometimes people are blocked from learning from others because of their envy or jealousy. This behaviour is self-defeating and does not enhance our self-worth. We can learn from others without comparing ourselves to them – we must not allow envy or jealousy to block us in this process. These feelings are often linked with childhood. Staying with them may help us to find out parts of our personal history. It may also free us to live more in the here-and-now.

- Sentence completion exercises can help us to become more self-aware and self-accepting. Finish the following sentences:

  a) I am beginning to feel…………………………………
  b) If I were more accepting of my anger………………
  c) If I were more accepting of my face…………………
  d) If I were more open about my needs…………………
  e) If I were less critical of myself………………………
  f) I am becoming more aware of………………………..
  g) I am becoming more accepting of……………………
  h) I am becoming more loving of ………………………
  i) I am becoming more understanding of………………

- We need to learn to protect ourselves against verbal abuse which is common in our society. How can we do it? The pain of verbal abuse goes deep into the self and affects us more than we realise. Look at the following questions:

  a) Was I verbally abused as a child? If so, how?
  b) What are the effects of such abuse on my relationships now?
  c) What can I do now to free myself of these effects?

It is important that we work through our past verbal abuses. They may not be as obvious as physical or sexual abuses and yet they have an enormous impact on us. We discover again another part of our personal history and we can learn from the past. This gives us hope and helps us to integrate our past painful experiences without having to repress them. We also learn to discover our vulnerable parts and aspects of our personality. It is equally important to know what to do when we experience verbal abuse in the present. Obviously, in this book I can only give you some hints.

a) Become aware of your vulnerable areas and that you are under attack. Many people do not recognize danger when it is there. They were told that they were too 'sensitive', or too 'childish'. They believed it and have become victims of attack. You need to become aware of the signs of verbal attack. If your emotion of anger is not repressed, you will feel anger when you are under verbal attack. Try to read people's facial expressions and tone of voice.

b) Become aware of the kind of attack. What 'weapons', does the attacker use? Some signs are obvious, such as loud voice, insulting words and unpleasant facial expressions. Others are more covert, such as flattering words, sarcastic or cynical remarks. They make us defenceless.

c) Make your defence fit the attack. You must choose an appropriate response, appropriate also to the level of attack. For minor attacks you must not come in with heavy 'guns'. For strong attacks 'enough is enough' may do the work.

d) Carry out your response. Verbal self-defence is a gentle art. It is a non-violent activity, a way of keeping peace. Thus women who have been conditioned to be 'nice' need to use this approach honestly. It is a way of maintaining good relationships and bringing out the best in the other person. It would be a great grace if in families both partners could use this approach. Many more families would survive.

Ask yourself:

- How do I understand love?
- Is love just a feeling or is it more than that?
- Do I really love myself?
- Are there aspects of myself which I cannot accept?
- How did I learn to hate some parts of myself?
- What were some of the messages I picked up as I grew up? Do they still rule my life? Do I feel I need to change some of these messages?
- How confident am I? What efforts have I made to grow in confidence?
- If I imagine myself being confident in whatever I do, then how does that affect my performance?
- Do I love people? If so, how do I show my love for them?
- What is my relationship with people from other cultures or religions?
- How well do I relate to men?
- How well do I relate to women?
- What is my relationship with children?
- What are some of my expectations of myself? Are they realistic? Are these the expectations my parents had for me? Do I want to change some of them?
- If I love somebody, do I expect love in return? What happens if I do not receive love in return?
- How conditional is my love for people? What happens to my love for them if the conditions are not met?
- How can I grow in love?
- Do I forgive people if they hurt me?
- Do I still greet people if they are nasty to me?

Conclusions

Many people have a wrong concept of love. The first important task for us is to learn what true love is. True love is unconditional and reaches out to all people. Love is a healing presence to a person without expecting anything in return. True love is found in imperfect people struggling to support each other. Only true love gives people the strength to go through all the painful experiences of growing together.

There are many ways we can learn to grow in love. First, we need to learn to accept ourselves. Our relationship with ourselves is the key to improving our relationships with others. Secondly, we need to acquire self-confidence by learning to improve our self-esteem. This will take patient practice. As we grow in love the whole atmosphere around us and within us will change and improve all our relationships.

Chapter three

The importance of trust in relationships

To trust or not to trust is something we learn in early childhood. Trust is a positive attitude towards oneself and others. If we do not learn it, we will struggle with relationships. However, our level of trust is a matter of degree. Some people are very trusting. Others are struggling to trust. Developing trust is usually a very slow process. It takes time. People have had mixed experiences in previous relationships. Some people may have been painfully let down. These people need time to learn to trust again. They will test you out to see whether they can trust you or not. They will reveal very little about themselves at the beginning. They are suspicious. We need to understand these people. We have to be non-judgemental when they share some negative aspects of themselves. Before they enter a deeper relationship with us they may want to know some personal details about us. We need to take their mistrust seriously and respond accordingly. If we do not want to share personal details with them we need to tell them and, if possible, give them a reason if we wish to continue the relationship.

To what degree have I learned to trust? Should I trust everybody? Do I trust myself? How stable is my trust? Is it easily shaken? Whom do I trust? Whom do I not trust? These are crucial questions. If I have learned to trust everybody indiscriminately, I must learn to distinguish whom I can trust. If I have learned to trust nobody, I must learn to discern whom I can trust.

What trust is not

Often we hear people say: "You can't trust men. You can't trust women". People who say this state more about themselves than about the opposite sex. They may have deep pain because of negative early childhood experiences. Trusting certain people means for them getting hurt. This wound needs to be healed before a person can enter a truly loving relationship. After divorce people may have a need to prove to themselves and others that they can relate well by quickly establishing a new relationship. Such relationships are usually short-lived.

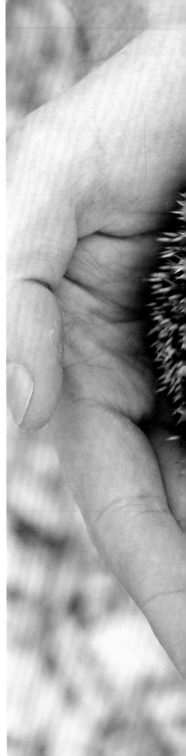

A deep love wound leads to fear of trusting. The people with such a wound may yearn for warmth, but as soon as they come closer to the person they love, they become afraid of being hurt again. They have learned to mistrust people. They always want to 'play it safe' and therefore they avoid taking risks. They are inclined to control others and come across as cold, rejecting, suspicious and often hostile. They are often afraid of authority, display feelings of superiority and show lack of respect for others.

Why have some people so little trust in themselves or in others? Often it comes from our learning and conditioning. What does an anxious mother say to a child as he/she goes off to school? Most likely she will say: "Be careful, darling." What is she really saying? "I am anxious that something may happen to you and I am not able to cope with that." She passes on to the child her lack of trust in her ability to cope. The child learns not to trust himself/herself. An anxious mother will say similar things in many other situations. As an adult, the person can change these messages in themselves and prudently try out situations in which they take calculated risks in trusting others.

What is true trust?

Trust is the foundation of human relationships. It is linked with creativity and personal growth. It is the glue which holds family, society and Church together. Healthy trust is the ability to distinguish between people on whom we can count and those on whom we cannot count, those on whom we can depend and those on whom we cannot depend, those in whom we can have faith and those in whom we cannot have faith, and act accordingly. There are people whom, for various reasons, we should not trust. It would be imprudent to share with them on a personal level. There are people whom we can trust and with whom we can share. We need to learn to distinguish between these two types of people. Obviously, there are many degrees of trustworthiness in both groups.

We need to have an idea of what healthy trust is before we can think about improving our relationships. We all have some understanding of trust from what we have learned in our family. We may have never questioned the notion of trust because this was built upon our childhood experience and remained with us till now. Let us take time to reflect upon what trust means for us and how we can improve our understanding of it.

Over many years of my life I have often had experiences in which trust was abused. For example, I gave a lecture and shared a personal experience which was very precious to me because I had gained a new insight. After I had shared it, it backfired and I came under attack from a couple of students. I learned painfully to be more cautious in sharing certain insights.

Ask yourself:
- Think of instances when your trust was betrayed. What did you learn from it?
- Did you decide not to trust anybody anymore?
- Did you learn to distinguish whom you can trust and with whom you can share appropriately?

Trusting people, respecting others and creating an atmosphere in which people can share safely.

The Oxford Dictionary describes respect as "admiration felt towards a person or thing that has good qualities or achievements". It states further that politeness arises from this. Respect fosters good relationships and is necessary for people who wish to spend quality time together and who admire each other. Mutual politeness is a necessary component of happy and trusting relationships.

People who trust believe in equality and cooperation with others. They are willing to take reasonable risks, are spontaneous and genuine. They feel free to say what they want to say. People can depend on them, since they are self-accountable and supportive of others. They relate with great empathy and warmth and understand the feelings of others. It becomes clearer to us that trust is at the foundation of human relationships. It develops gradually and requires continual efforts to maintain it, particularly when people suffer from abusive relationships. This is part of our society.

Trusting persons do not hide behind roles but respond to the uniqueness of other people by mutual sharing. They foster self-growth and growth of others and are willing to share of self. They have the ability to talk truthfully about themselves which is essential for effective communication. The more the two people know about each other, the better they can communicate with each other. Every person has a store of experiences, emotions, thoughts and ideas. Trust helps us to know and be known by others provided we are willing and able to self-disclose appropriately.

There are many obstacles to personal sharing. Many people are afraid to share because they fear they might not be accepted if the other person knows certain things about them. They may be afraid of rejection. They may feel unworthy. They may be afraid of being misunderstood or afraid of not expressing themselves clearly. They need to replace fear by prudent trust. In a threatening or new situation, it would be imprudent to share too much about ourselves. Part of learning to share more is to create an atmosphere of trust in which both can share without too much fear.

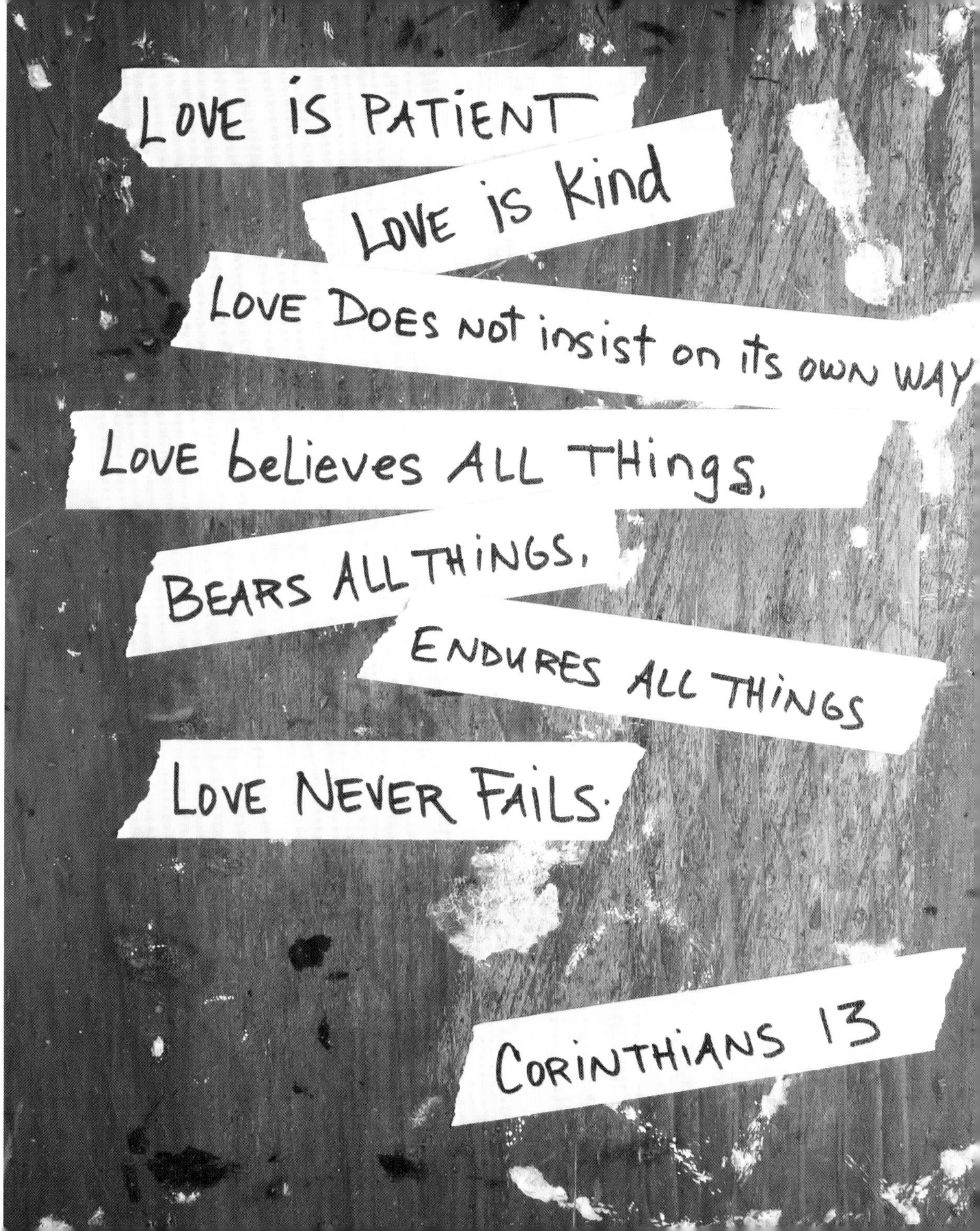

LOVE IS PATIENT

LOVE is Kind

LOVE DOES not insist on its own WAY

LOVE believes ALL THings,

BEARS ALL THINGS,

ENDURES ALL THINGS

LOVE NEVER FAILS.

CORINTHIANS 13

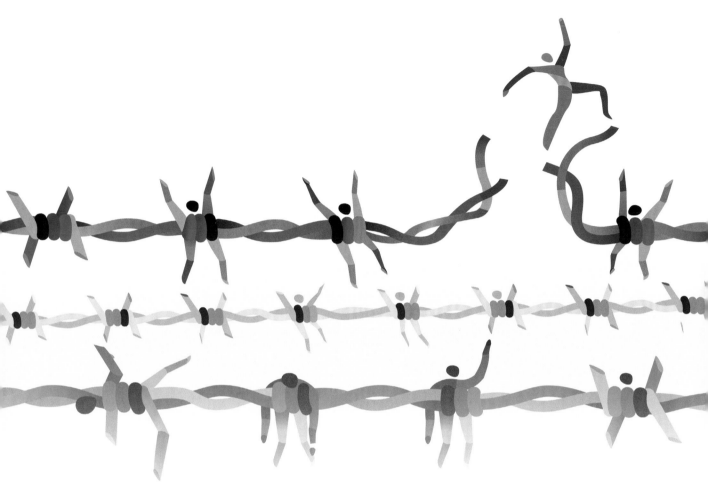

For some people personal sharing may be difficult because they were never encouraged to talk about themselves when they were children. Others may have been the constant centre of attention and could say anything they wanted at any time. They need to learn to contain their habit of sharing all the time about themselves. They may find it difficult to listen to others. Then listening is their area for personal development.

All these positive behaviours, which we can learn at any age, foster healthy relationships and focus on the 'here-and-now'. People change their inappropriate patterns of behaviour in the present situation. Trusting people are positive in their outlook because they are dealing with the present situation and not responding with patterns of behaviour from the past.

When we put too much trust in others, it can ruin our life and our business. When we lack trust, we may never fully develop our potential. It is difficult, but important, to find the middle way between the two extremes. Hopefully we will gradually learn to find the right amount of trust for every given situation and person.

When trust is betrayed, hurt and anger develop in people and also a fear of ever trusting again. Many people have gone through such experiences and so struggle with relationships. On the one hand they yearn for a deeper relationship; on the other hand the moment they come closer to the other person, the fear of abuse or rejection, or both, are activated and they back off. They try to protect themselves from being hurt again. They feel vulnerable when they come too close. "Too close" differs from person to person. We need to have patience and understanding with such people and allow them to withdraw until they feel safe.

Only in an atmosphere of warmth and safety will people open up. People do not want to risk being hurt again. Thus we defend ourselves against love itself. We avoid intimate relationships and friendships and prefer the safety of casual acquaintances. However, we need to learn to go beyond that and take reasonable risks to trust and trust again. People use many means of protecting themselves. We can foster customer and shopkeeper relationships. We may enrol on a course and get engaged in a student teacher relationship. Is this the reason why some people follow one course after another? Some people take refuge in a tenant to landlord relationship or employee to boss. People differ greatly and are often not aware of why they foster such relationships and avoid deeper ones. These surface relationships are safer; the person does not become too vulnerable. Some people may reduce others to a mere object to be used for personal satisfaction.

People may ask themselves: "How much should I find out about the other person and how much should I let them know about myself? It may be prudent to ask these questions or it may be a defence to protect myself. If I allow myself to be drawn into a risky relationship too soon, what will happen to my shaky self?"

People often move between respect and suspicion of the other person. Trust can give way to suspicion. People change, and then we find how little trust they merited. Once trust is tarnished, it is difficult to restore it to its original beauty.

Learning to trust is essential for improving our relationships

We need to learn to distinguish between people whom we can trust and people whom we can't trust. All of us come across both types of people. Trust develops slowly. Instant trust lacks discernment. How will it stand up to pressure? Let us compare the process of developing trust to peeling an onion. First one has to remove the outer layers, then one can go deeper and deeper. The outer layers provide a protection.

The first step is to test out, then we can begin to trust. The proverb tells us: "If you trust before you try, you may repent before you die." We need to learn wise distrust. It is the parent of security. However, where there is no trust, there is no love. Many people are afraid of betrayal and therefore they distrust each other.

One way of finding out whether you can trust a person is to share areas of emotional sensitivity. Such areas are: past experiences, concerns about physical appearance, feelings of rejection, anger, envy or jealousy and so on. Suppose the other person uses these matters against you, then you will not share more about yourself and trust will suffer. If the other person respects your sensitivities you can reveal deeper emotional vulnerabilities. Trust, caring and respect will grow and enable you to share more personal and embarrassing parts of who you are. You are reasonably sure that the disclosure will not be used against you.

Another way trust can develop in a relationship is that both share current personal difficulties and worries. This mutual sharing produces protection and fosters open communication. Frequently people who experience a serious crisis together share deep matters and feel very close.

Yet another way to discern the level of trust is to observe the other person and see whether there is a discrepancy between what he or she says and what he or she does. Will the other person stand by his or her word? Has he or she let you down once, twice or many times?

There are many forms of exploitation in relationships of which neither party may be aware. They are so used to exploiting and to being exploited, that it takes them time to find out that such a relationship is disastrous. For example, one person gives frequent gifts to her friend. The receiver does not want to return presents. They never talk about it. After some time the person who gives presents will see that her unexpressed expectations are not fulfilled and cannot understand the other person. She would never do such a thing.

Often couples ignore potential problem areas. They do not discuss important issues for fear that it would destroy their 'good' relationship. They do not want to look at their relationship and see where it is going. But people need to check out early in their relationship their assumptions about each other and the expectations they have for each other, to find out whether they are meant for each other or not. They need to share their feelings and honestly ask questions about their relationship so that they know where they stand and whether they can withstand the tension of their relationship. Both can learn more about their relationship and avoid disappointment later on.

People have a desire to be understood and appreciated for who they really are. To achieve this, they need gradually to let down their facades and show their true colours. This can lead to a much deeper level of relating. Intimacy blossoms as a result of sharing deeply and being understood and accepted 'warts and all'.

Ask yourself:

Trust in people and in God
- ♦ Do I trust myself?
- ♦ Do I trust others?
- ♦ Do I trust men?
- ♦ Do I trust women?
- ♦ Do I trust authority?
- ♦ Do I trust God?

Trust in my abilities
- ♦ What can I do well?
- ♦ Which areas did I not develop?
- ♦ Are there some areas I would like to develop?
- ♦ Am I aware of my abilities?
- ♦ What are some of the areas I would need to develop to improve the quality of my life?

Trust in others: valid or blind?
- ♦ Do I trust in the ability of other people?
- ♦ Do I trust my doctor?
- ♦ Do I trust my dentist?
- ♦ Do I trust my nurse?
- ♦ Do I trust my boss?
- ♦ Do I trust my husband or wife?

Trust in men or women: my generalisations
- ♦ Are there some men or women whom I trust?
- ♦ Who are those men or women?
- ♦ What reasons do I have for trusting them?
- ♦ What reasons do I have for not trusting other men or women?
- ♦ Have I learnt to distinguish between those whom I trust and those whom I don't trust?
- ♦ Am I ready to seek out men and women whom I am able to trust, and to recognise men and women whom I can't or shouldn't trust?

Trust in authority
- ♦ Are there some people in authority whom I trust?
- ♦ If yes, what are their characteristics and why do I trust them?
- ♦ If not, why have I not yet learnt that there are trustworthy people in authority
- ♦ Do I try to avoid all authority figures?
- ♦ Have I generalised, from my childhood experiences, not to trust any authority figures?
- ♦ Would I like to change this attitude and learn to trust authority figures who are deserving of my trust?

Trust in God
- ♦ Do I trust God always? If not why not?
- ♦ Would I like to change that?
- ♦ What are the advantages of trusting God?
- ♦ What are the advantages of not trusting God?
- ♦ What would my life be like if I trusted God?
- ♦ Would trusting God improve the quality of my life?

Conclusions

A healthy ability to trust is an essential characteristic of good relationships. Some people acquire it as children, others struggle to ascertain whether they can trust people or not. Everybody can learn to trust in a healthy way. There are many degrees of trusting. Some people trust too much and others trust too little. We need to learn to discern whom we can trust. As our trust matures, our relationships will profit by it and growth will take place.

Trusting people have great respect for each other and build up an atmosphere in which they can share sensitive matters. Usually trust develops gradually and needs to be maintained or restored after we have encountered abusive relationships. In trusting relationships people develop and mature. They overcome the fears of sharing about themselves in a warm and caring atmosphere of healthy relationships. A great amount of understanding and patience is needed to develop healthy relationships. Many people need to learn to trust again by mutual sharing in a prudent way.

Chapter four

The importance of good communication in relationships

What is not good communication?

Often people want to communicate in order to express their anger towards a person for whatever may have happened. They want to get rid of their anger. This process may be unconscious. For example, George has worked hard all day at the office. The boss corrects him for some aspect of his work in an irate way. He comes home with his anger, which he did not dare to express to the boss, so when he arrives back home he displaces it on to his wife, who has prepared his favourite supper. "Why do you always cook the same food? Can't we have more variety?" he shouts. He had forgotten that last week, when he was in a good mood, he had told her that he liked this dish.

Often we offload our anger on to people who are no threat to us. We feel safe with them. If you are the recipient of such anger, keep in mind that this is actually a sign that the person trusts you. Obviously, this kind of communication is normally not very helpful because the person who is the recipient of the anger is at least confused, if not hurt and blocked in further communication. A painful silence may be the result of such events, until one of the two dares to break the silence and to resume the conversation again.

Another form of unfruitful communication is when two people talk to each other without listening. Both have the urge to talk and are not ready to listen. At the end of such outpouring both are exhausted and drained. Since this happens without awareness, they don't know why they feel so tired and neither has heard what the other has said. These are habitual behaviours and can be changed, provided the two become aware of it.

At such times both may feel frustrated, because they sense the other person did not understand what he or she was saying. Instead of building each other up, they are pulling each other down, most likely unintentionally. They may even feel angry, because they were not listened to. Many people who were not listened to in their past have a deep-rooted desire to be listened to and have very strong feelings from the past when this does not happen.

Another form of poor communication exists when one person constantly asks closed questions such as: "Are you married? Is your wife still alive? Where were you last night? Do you have a girlfriend? Do you keep your promises?" Some people are very inquisitive and ask one question after another with the result that the other person will make an excuse and leave. They do not want to be interrogated. Such questions can trigger strong feelings from the past, such as when they went out for a dance and next morning father or mother asked them: "When did you come home? Who were you with?" etc.

One particular form of bad communication is when one person constantly uses the word 'why'. The other person may experience the conversation as an interrogation with all the negative feelings that go with such questioning. People acquire these habits without realising it. However, they block healthy communication with its flow of energy. Once we are aware of this, we can change it.

Communication is impaired when a person constantly corrects or ridicules the statement the other person makes. They feel put down and avoid the person, who may simply have learnt the habit of being critical and is unaware of its impact. This is an asset in given circumstances such as editing an article for a newspaper. Anything we have learned is also a resource, if we use it in the right situation. Most things we learned in childhood can also be an asset if we use them in the right context.

Some people are shy and find it difficult to get involved in a conversation. However, we can gently draw them out of their isolation, which blocks them from communicating, by asking simple questions that will put them at ease.

Ask yourself:

♦ Do I listen to people?
♦ Do I feed back to people that I understand them?
♦ Are there frequent misunderstandings between me and my friend, between me and my boss, between me and my partner?
♦ Am I too shy to say what I want to say?

What is good communication?

I am sure you have met people whom you admired for their communication skills. Have you ever thought that you could become like that person? We learn to communicate as we grow up. Very often we imitate our parents in the way they communicate with people. We learn it from them and copy them, just as we do in other areas of development such as walking, eating, expression of emotions and other aspects of life.

An essential part of good communication is active listening. Many people find it difficult to listen and therefore they are struggling to have a healthy way of communicating. We can learn to become good listeners. We can also learn to respond to others in a constructive way.

Good communication is like a dance. Both people are tuned into each other as the conversation flows. At the end of such encounters, both feel refreshed and enriched. They are energized. They want to be together. They want to talk more and more often with each other.

A few years ago when I was travelling from Rome to London, there was a man next to me who was reading a book on how to handle teenagers. I had a desire to get involved in a conversation. I asked an open question: "What do you think about our young people?" I chose this topic because I saw that he was interested in it. Intentionally I kept my question as wide as possible and was ready for any answer. In no time we were involved in a deep conversation about teenagers and how he struggled with his own son and daughter. The time passed very quickly and we arrived in London recognizing a potential friendship. We even talked about how we could meet again.

In good communication both sides are attentive to each other. They are proactive in finding out what the other person wants to say, and facilitate the sharing through their whole non-verbal and verbal communication. Both know that the other person wants to be understood just as each one of them has a desire to be understood.

Good communication comes always out of love. God, who is Love, gave us this gift of language so that we can share our authentic love, which is the centre of our being, with others. My intention in good communication is to build up the other person, not to put him or her down, in whatever I say. If my motive is love for the other person, then the communication will most likely be constructive. I will find the right words and the right tone of voice, because it comes out of my deep centre of love.

Both listening and responding to what the person has said are important. In responding we need to communicate that we have understood the other person before we introduce another topic. Some people have a great need to be understood. They may have never felt understood in childhood. It is important that we feed back to them that we have understood what they have said. We can echo back what we have heard. We can also feed back to them the emotions which we picked up in what they said. In good communication it is essential that both sides feel understood.

How can we improve our communication?

We need to observe ourselves to become aware of the way we communicate, how we listen to people, what emotions we experience as we communicate. Awareness is essential. Without awareness nothing will change. Once we are aware, then we can decide what we want to change in our communication. We might decide to listen more before we respond. We might decide not to throw our anger at people, but to get rid of the anger in a constructive way e.g. by doing something energetic like running, digging in the garden, cleaning the house etc. before we talk to a person. We might decide to share our feelings with the person, so that he or she understands us better. We might decide to stop our habit of ridiculing people.

We might decide not to use the word 'why' so frequently. Awareness is key to good communication. Old habits can be changed, provided we are aware of them and want to change them. We do not have to be fixed in our way of communicating for the rest of our lives.

We also need to look at the behaviour patterns we have acquired from childhood and which are no longer constructive or appropriate in our present situation. We may have learned to cry when we feel angry. We were not allowed to show anger in our family because mother could not cope with this strong emotion. As an adult I can allow myself to feel anger and use the energy of the anger in a constructive way. We are no longer helpless children, but adults. We have acquired many skills. Now we have to decide to use these skills appropriately.

Good body language plays a major part in improving our communication.

Body language or nonverbal communication plays a major part in our relationships. Not only what we say but how we communicate nonverbally has an immense impact on people: facial expressions, eye movements, nods, gestures and postures are all part of body language.

Some researchers say that 10% of our communication is words, 40% is tone of voice and 50% is visual or body communication. If we want to improve our communication, we need to be aware of our nonverbal communication and change much of it. This can be great fun, but also a powerful tool for having better relationships. Ideally, our words, tone of voice and body language should give the same message. This is congruent communication. You look, sound and speak honestly and genuinely. It is essential that you mean what you say, and say what you mean.

Shyness or embarrassment may interfere with your communication because it produces physical clumsiness. You may say to your guests: "I am pleased with your visit." Your shyness may produce nonverbal communication such as a weak handshake which contradicts the statement.

Body language is the most revealing form of communication. I may say that I love you, but the tone of voice and the body language express the opposite. The outcome of such communication may be confusion. I remember many years ago a friend told me: "You have a very stern look which contradicts your verbal messages." I have worked on that and try to come across the way I want to come across. Sometimes the message needs to be more serious, sometimes it needs to be more caring and understanding, but it always needs to be loving, even, and especially, when we have to do caring confrontation. Caring confrontation needs to be used when we have to correct a person for their destructive behaviour. The person who confronts must communicate from their centre of love and not anger.

Usually people are not aware of their body language. We learn it in childhood by copying our parents or parent-substitutes. Part of improving our relationships has to do with becoming aware of our nonverbal communication. Once we are aware of it, then we can decide to change it and acquire different nonverbal patterns of communication. As we learn the different aspects of body language, we learn to "read" other people's. This will affect our relationships in the family, workplace, school, sport and wherever we are with people.

Since communication is so important for our relationships, it is a pity that we do not learn to pay attention to it at school or in the family. Many books have been written on this topic. It is not the purpose of this book to explore it in depth, but to point out its importance and to stress that body language is learned and can be changed so that we become better communicators.

As children we used body language to get what we wanted long before we could speak. Not only our crying caught the attention of our parents, but also our facial expressions, the movements of our legs, arms and body were powerful tools of communication. Let us just think of a temper tantrum. How much is verbal communication and how much is nonverbal communication? Which one affects us more; the crying or the movements? Of which do we get more frightened when an adult throws a temper tantrum? I have often observed it in therapy groups. You may have seen it in the workplace, at school or in your family.

You may like to become more aware of the display of body language, such as stamping, door slamming, clenched fists, folded arms, shrugging of shoulders, shutting or rolling of eyes, head bowed, finger pointing, head-shaking, hands on hips, staring, just to mention a few.

As people get more used to reading body language, they will find out many things from their observations. The body may indicate that the person fancies you. Often we notice through body language that a person is insecure. Some people can detect that a person is lying. Other people display their competitiveness. From the body language alone we can pick up many important messages which will affect our relationships with people. Our nonverbal communication greatly affects the way we are perceived by others.

Improving our communication with others needs to start with improving our communication with ourselves.

Many people are not aware how destructive they are with themselves. They are their own worst enemy. It has much to do with the way they communicate with themselves constantly. They would need to observe their self-talk. How often do they call themselves stupid, worthless, insensitive, slow, foolish, silly, ugly, too tall, too small, too fat, too thin, irresponsible, dull and other negative labels?

This self-talk has become a habit and they believe that they are stupid, foolish, ugly, dull and worthless. They never question this. Now they have to dismantle this negative critic and develop a more realistic attitude and language for who they really are. This negative self-talk has damaged them. However, they can repair the damage by becoming more positive and realistic about themselves. They live in the past. They need to learn to live in the present. They need to become aware of their positive sides and foster them. This will beneficially affect all their relationships.

As a Christian I know that I am made in the image and likeness of God. I also know that the essence of God is love. Therefore, there is a kernel of love in me. When I pray the 'Our Father' I become aware that God is my Father and that I am a child of God. For me this is the deepest layer of my identity and I feel very privileged, grateful and happy about it. I am aware that I don't always live up to the standards God has set me in the ten commandments and the Beatitudes, but I also know that God forgives me my faults and shortcomings and I never cease to be a child of God. My fundamental relationship with God has an influence on all my relationships. I try to love all people and relate positively to all people as God wants me to. I pray for all people.

Ask yourself:

- How do I communicate with myself?
- Do I constantly put myself down?
- What frequent adjectives do I use for myself?
- As a Christian, am I aware that God is my Father and that I am a child of God?
- How does my relationship with God influence other relationships?
- What do I consider good communication with God?

Write down the answer to the following questions:

- Have you now detected some of the reasons for your misunderstandings?
- What have you decided to do about it?
- Would it be prudent to discuss this with your friend, boss or partner?
- How does your way of communication block your relationships?
- How can your communication improve your relationships?
- Imagine what your relationships would be like if you worked on improving your communication.
- How do you communicate with God, if at all?
- How do your emotions interfere with your communication?
- What are your assets with regard to good communication?
- Do you use these resources frequently?

Conclusions

If we want to improve our relationships we need to become good communicators. This implies that we need both to listen and to respond. Some people may not have the necessary skills for good communication. However, they can learn them. Often the emotion of anger interferes with good communication. People can learn to manage their anger constructively. We can all improve our communication in many ways. The first step is to become aware of the weaknesses in our communication and then decide to change them one by one.

It is not only words we use when we communicate but also our body language. Both affect our relationships. We have acquired habits of verbal and nonverbal communication. Some of them are good and some of them need changing to improve our relationships.

If we want to improve our communication with others, we need to start to improve it with ourselves. Often in our self-talk we are our own worst enemy. We need to become our own best friend.

The important role emotions play
in relationship

Emotions: a curse or a blessing?

We cannot overestimate the importance of the emotions in relating to others. Joy, for example, enormously contributes to the wellbeing of our relationships. Emotions also play a major part in the breakdown of relationships. A hurtful word often becomes the seed for revenge. How many people have been killed because of jealousy? Some people in their rage can destroy furniture. Emotions have had a bad reputation because of their abuse. Actually, the emotions are a gift from God, just as the body is a gift from God. Both can be used constructively or destructively. Most of us use them both ways. The question is: "How can we become more constructive with our emotions and allow them to fulfil the function for which they were created, according to God's plan in our lives." Life without emotions would be very dull. Joy and excitement would not be part of our life.

Early learning of emotional behaviour

Early in our lives we learn how to deal with our emotions and develop behaviour patterns which are either healthy or unhealthy. Many people carry on these patterns for the rest of their lives. Some will change certain patterns, because they notice that they disturb their relationships. For each one of us there are many great opportunities to keep on growing in how we can use our emotions constructively. The following are some illustrations of various emotions.

Anger

I have worked on anger for over thirty years and I still discover areas and ways in which I can use this emotion more constructively. If we desire to grow in love, we have to learn to use this emotion positively. Some people have learned to repress their anger which then goes into passive aggressive behaviour, which is unconscious, but inconveniences other people. They may try to cheer people up and make a joke, but it backfires because of the sting in the joke. People try to avoid them because they feel ill-at-ease with the joking person. Nobody really knows why they are uncomfortable. Other people have learned in childhood to act out their anger either by shouting, arguing, or even physical attack. Everybody is aware of such angry people and we try to keep away to avoid becoming the target of their anger.

Both people who repress their anger and people who act it out need to work on it. The former have to learn to feel the anger, name it, own it and use it constructively. The latter group of people may need to contain their anger and learn how to vent it in constructive ways such as digging in the garden, cleaning the house, going for walks and many other activities.

Most of us probably repress anger sometimes; it then goes into passive aggressive behaviour and at other times we become inappropriately aggressive in our conversations with people. We may even express anger towards other people who are not the real target of our anger but are a substitute, because we feel free to do it with that person. Some teenagers may be very pleasant with their peers but become quite aggressive with their parents. Parents need to learn not to get upset and see it as a sign of intimacy. They trust their parents to go on loving them even if they air their anger; they do not yet trust their friends to do the same.

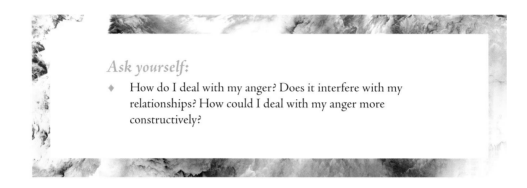

Ask yourself:

♦ How do I deal with my anger? Does it interfere with my relationships? How could I deal with my anger more constructively?

Fear

The function of anger is to protect ourselves after fear has alerted us to danger. Fear is a warning signal to be careful because there is danger ahead. The danger may be physical, such as a person threatening to attack us. It may be a psychological threat to our self-concept. It could also be a spiritual threat where somebody is attacking our religious beliefs. Often, once fear is triggered, anger comes up to give us the energy to protect ourselves. Sometimes people freeze when they are afraid and can't move or protect themselves. They have learned to suppress their anger. They need to allow themselves to feel the anger and to use the energy of that anger constructively so that they prevent harm to themselves or others.

Many people suffer from fears which they learned when they were small children. As I explained earlier I learned to fear dogs and was so afraid that I would avoid going to a house where there was a dog, but I unlearned what I had learned as a child with regard to dogs and am no longer afraid of them. In fact, I love them now.

Some people are afraid of spiders, others of mice, others of snakes and any other animal depending on what they learned as children. What we have learned we can unlearn. People are not dominated just by fear of animals, but also by fear of things. Some are afraid of water, others of the dark. I am afraid of heights. Some people are afraid of the unknown such as death or the future in general.

Many fears dominate people's lives. It is important that we become aware of ours. We may often deny them. Once we are aware of what they are, we can prioritize them and start working on them in small steps. Many people have already learned to free themselves from some fears. How did they do it? Usually when we are afraid of something, we try to avoid it. Now we have to learn to relate to the object of fear in small, manageable doses. By following small steps of relating to the object of fear, we become aware that what we learned as children was not the full picture, but only one aspect of it. As we get a clear and fuller picture of the object of fear, we learn to distinguish when it is healthy to be afraid and when it is unhealthy. We desensitize ourselves by relating to the object of the fear. The past slowly loses its grip on the present. We learn to relate to people, animals and the environment in a realistic way.

Fear of authority is very common. Some people are afraid of their boss. Others are afraid of the police. Many people are afraid of the Catholic Church as a moral authority and fight it. Ask yourself: "Of what authority am I afraid?" There are people who are afraid of doctors, quite a few are afraid of dentists. We can ask ourselves: "Where and when did I learn this fear?" Understanding the origin of our fears will help us to deal with them.

Many fears are a means of protecting us from harm. If we would not be afraid of a dangerous dog, we might be attacked. The fear signals to us that there is a danger for which we need to prepare ourselves. If we had no fear of any snake, a poisonous snake might bite us and we could die. There is such a thing as a healthy fear which we need to preserve.

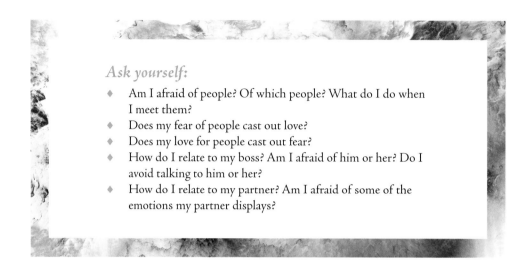

Ask yourself:

- Am I afraid of people? Of which people? What do I do when I meet them?
- Does my fear of people cast out love?
- Does my love for people cast out fear?
- How do I relate to my boss? Am I afraid of him or her? Do I avoid talking to him or her?
- How do I relate to my partner? Am I afraid of some of the emotions my partner displays?

Anxiety

Some people are anxious nearly all the time and over many things. Just as we learn fear, so we learn anxiety. Fear is easier to detect, because we know what we fear. It may be an animal, a person, an exam, etc. Anxiety is often free floating. We don't know why we are anxious. When I was forty years old I had a great deal of anxiety. After some time I found out that it had to do with my state of health. It became clear that I was anxious because I struggled with a lack of energy. I did not know what to do. How did I deal with this anxiety? As I reflected upon it, the severity of it indicated to me that it might be going back to childhood experiences.

At the age of three I had a high temperature and was seeing snakes on the ceiling. I was so unwell that one night my mother called my siblings because she thought I was going to die. Happily, I recovered. Once I realised that my anxiety had to do with that event in my childhood, the severity of the anxiety was greatly reduced. In addition to this insight, I realised that, in spite of my lack of energy, I could manage what I was doing. I said to myself: "If it stays like this, you will manage the workload. If it gets better, you can take on more work. If it gets worse, you can reduce the present workload." This helped me to deal with my anxiety. Part of the huge anxiety was from the past and the rest I worked out in the here-and-now.

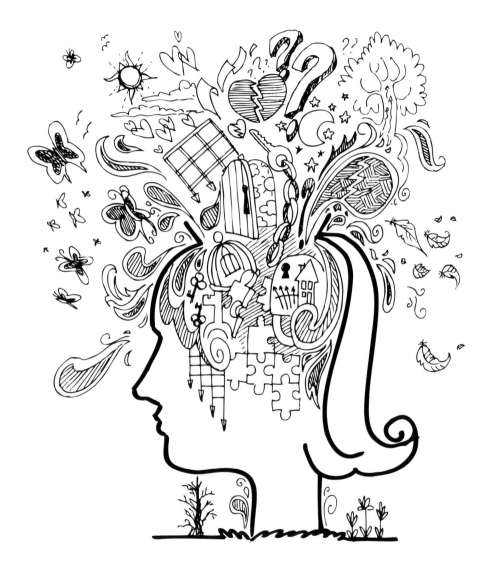

A certain amount of anxiety can be healthy. For example, if I have to sit for an examination, I feel anxious. The anxiety tells me I have to prepare for my exam. I start preparing and my anxiety goes down. If I did not feel any anxiety, I might not do anything and fail the exam. The anxiety motivates us to do something. It would not be good for us not to feel a certain amount of anxiety. However, we must not let it take over.

I may be anxious when I meet new people. If I avoid meeting new people, it interferes with the richness of my relationships and I keep myself limited to just a few. I can learn to deal with the anxiety by preparing myself to meet a new person. In childhood I may not have had the opportunity to meet new people. My parents may have been overprotective of me. As an adult I have the chance to get to know new people and be enriched by that experience. Each new relationship widens our horizon of what it means to be a human being.

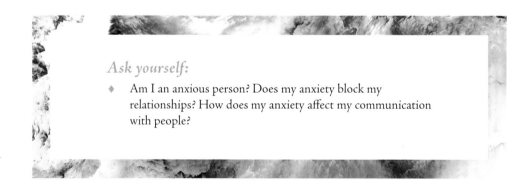

Ask yourself:

♦ Am I an anxious person? Does my anxiety block my relationships? How does my anxiety affect my communication with people?

Guilt

When we experience guilt, we can ask ourselves: "Have I done something wrong? What is it?" Healthy guilt feelings help us to make good what we have done wrong. For example, I may have hurt my friend by using harsh words and now I feel guilty. I can apologize and say that I am sorry and try to repair the hurt I have caused. Guilt helps us to maintain good relationships.

However, not all guilt feelings are healthy. Some of our guilt feelings go back to childhood. Many people feel guilty when they feel angry. They were taught that anger is a sin. If they feel anger now, they feel guilty. These are irrational guilt feelings and may interfere with good relationships.

In my relationships I can also learn not to allow others to inculcate guilt feelings in me and in that way to control me. Children learn that if they blame others, they get away with what they did. We carry on this behaviour pattern as adults and keep on blaming others for our mistakes. Our relationships with others deteriorate. People don't like to be blamed for things they did not do. A few weeks ago I was driving my car down the main road when a lady drove out of a side road and ran into my car. There was very little damage done to either car, as I noticed her coming at the last minute and applied the brakes. I got out of my car and went to speak to her. She said to me: "You are lucky you got away with it"; obviously wanting to blame me. I had strong immediate reactions to this, but took on neither the blame nor the guilt – they didn't belong to me.

People often try to dominate us by inculcating guilt feelings in us. We may have to learn to protect ourselves from that behaviour. You may have learned to allow them to do this to you because your parents protected you and you never acquired the skill to protect yourself. Life is all about learning new skills to survive and prosper.

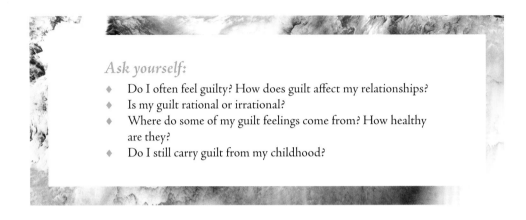

Ask yourself:

- Do I often feel guilty? How does guilt affect my relationships?
- Is my guilt rational or irrational?
- Where do some of my guilt feelings come from? How healthy are they?
- Do I still carry guilt from my childhood?

Shyness

Shyness seems to be a problem for many people at some stage in their life. For some it can be a mental handicap as incapacitating as a physical disability. Shyness makes it difficult for us to meet new people, to make friends, to enjoy potentially good experiences. A shy person finds it hard to speak up for his or her rights. They seem to be unable to express their opinions and values. Shyness makes it arduous to think clearly and to communicate effectively. Shy people are afraid of potentially emotionally threatening people like strangers, authorities and members of the opposite sex. They are inclined to remain silent.

Shyness means different things to different people. The frequency of shyness varies from culture to culture. Shyness has also a positive side. Some people like it because it implies favourable aspects like 'reserved', 'modest' and 'unassuming'. It makes a person appear introspective. Often shy people stand back, observe and then act deliberately. They can avoid many interpersonal conflicts. Some shy people may be considered as good listeners. Shyness increases a person's privacy.

We learn shyness as children. We may have copied one of our parents who was shy. There are many ways to acquire this emotion and allow it to rule our lives. It interferes with our relationships in many ways. We may not dare to say things which

we want to say. We may not dare to do things which we are well able to do. We may have few friends and feel very lonely.

A shy person can learn to overcome their shyness by efforts to do and say things which they want to do or say. They need to discern, so that when they do or say things, it will be successful. The success will encourage them to repeat this behaviour and slowly they learn that they can do it and overcome their shyness. They may need to learn how to communicate, what to communicate and why to communicate. Shy people may have distorted perceptions of what human relationships are all about.

Many shy people have low self-esteem. They avoid any situation that may be potentially embarrassing. They isolate themselves from other people and try to keep a low profile. If they want to change their behaviour they can learn to go out to people and not to isolate themselves. They need to take many such small steps to get out of their old habits and acquire new behaviours which will take time and need patience. Shyness can be successfully overcome by understanding it, building up our self-esteem and improving our social skills.

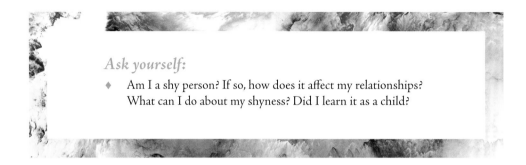

Ask yourself:

♦ Am I a shy person? If so, how does it affect my relationships? What can I do about my shyness? Did I learn it as a child?

Jealousy

Jealousy differs from envy. In a loving relationship, jealousy involves three parties: the person who loves another person and a third person who stirs up anxiety in the loving person. The loving person feels insecure with regard to the affection of the person she or he loves. Will they lose this affection because of the third person coming into the relationship? Envy involves only two parties. Jealous people want to possess the other person, whereas envious persons compare themselves to others.

Jealousy is an emotion which we experience when we have not enough trust in ourselves. Since many people lack trust in themselves, they will experience jealousy when somebody threatens their relationship with friends, partners, bosses etc. It is very common in romantic relationships. It is the cause of marital breakdown, of spousal violence and many murders.

We can distinguish between healthy and unhealthy jealousy. Healthy jealousy will foster relationships while unhealthy jealousy will destroy them. Healthy jealousy will stimulate constructive communication about boundaries, rights and wishes. It also shows how capable people are of love. Jealousy can be a sign of love. Unhealthy jealousy leads to anguish and persecution fantasies. When jealousy becomes too intense it is often contaminated by painful childhood experiences.

We have to acknowledge jealousy, not suppress it. Full awareness of jealousy will help us to understand it and then to control it. We may need to challenge our irrational beliefs and assumptions. We can improve our communication skills. We can negotiate what is acceptable and what is not acceptable behaviour with others. Jealous people may need to improve their self-esteem. They may need to resolve issues of childhood that lead to unhealthy jealousy.

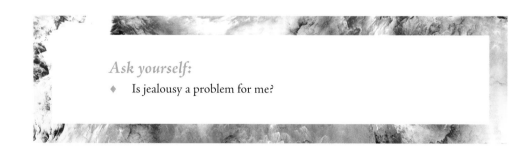

Ask yourself:

♦ Is jealousy a problem for me?

Envy

Envy is an overwhelming desire to own what another person has. Envy is a frequent companion of people in our time, because we have become very individualistic. A Danish proverb says: "If envy were a fever, all the world would be ill." We notice that somebody has things which we do not have. We envy him or her. It is linked with our values. If we value material things above all else, we feel envy when others have what we do not have. If holidays are most important for us, we may envy the person who can afford better and longer holidays.

By being envious we are the ones who suffer. We will never be happy and satisfied because there will always be somebody else with more who can afford things we cannot. Envious eyes see things which other people will not see and they suffer the lack of it. They feel inferior and will never be satisfied. Envy makes life miserable and destroys contentment. Envious people are often aggressive. They have little understanding of human nature and blame others for their lack of success. Envy interferes with relationships. Some envious people even enjoy the suffering and pain of others.

Envious people are frequently dissatisfied with life. They need to build up their self-esteem. This will most likely lessen the envy. They may become aware that they can be happy without having everything.

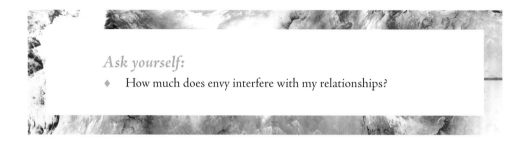

Ask yourself:

♦   How much does envy interfere with my relationships?

Hurt

We all feel hurt at certain times, particularly when we are tired. People may say something or do something and we feel hurt. At other times the same person may say the same things or do the same things and we do not feel hurt. When we are tired, we are inclined to interpret things more negatively.

People may stop communicating when they are hurt. Some people sulk when they are hurt but do not share the reasons for it. Hurt people may indirectly criticise or punish the other person. As they think about the hurt, they are inclined to exaggerate, to think that the other person does not care for them or hates them. We often make monsters of people who hurt us by breaking off all contact with them and fantasising about them negatively. Past hurts often contaminate the present hurt.

The person may have learnt this behaviour pattern in the family and can change it now. Hurt people should communicate their feelings directly to the person who hurt them in a loving way: "Our relationship is important for me, that is why I want to share my feelings with you." This will sensitise the other person about the effects of their talk or actions on others. If both listen to each other, it will deepen their relationship. The hurt person may become aware of the exaggeration of the hurt story and may see it more realistically. Both can gain by their caring communication.

The hurt person needs to acknowledge the hurt and see it as a problem to be solved. He or she needs to identify what hurts him or her most and look at that.

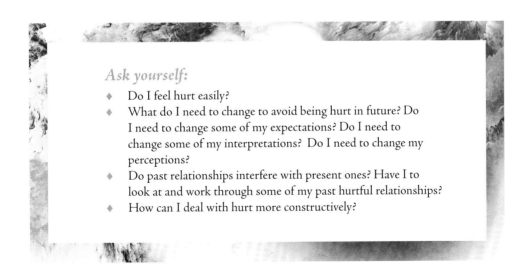

Ask yourself:
- ◆ Do I feel hurt easily?
- ◆ What do I need to change to avoid being hurt in future? Do I need to change some of my expectations? Do I need to change some of my interpretations? Do I need to change my perceptions?
- ◆ Do past relationships interfere with present ones? Have I to look at and work through some of my past hurtful relationships?
- ◆ How can I deal with hurt more constructively?

Shame

Shame is loss of face. If it is intensified, it can lead to despair. The emotion of shame is highly disturbing to the self and central to an unhealthy sense of identity. It can be the source of low self-esteem and lessen our self-image. It leads to a poor self-concept and even to a negative body-image. It fosters self-doubt and undermines our security and confidence. It diminishes our feeling of belonging and becomes an obstacle to intimacy. It is an affront to human dignity and is the breeding ground of loneliness, alienation, inferiority, depression and perfectionism. Shame involves the whole self. It reveals the inner self.

Shame is an emotion which restricts our lives considerably. It can stop us from taking any risks, but can also prevent us from doing things we would later regret. A person who feels no shame has no conscience. Have you ever thought, "This person should be ashamed of himself or herself"? Some people are ashamed of their poverty. But poverty is not shameful, however being ashamed of it is.

Shame is one of the greatest obstacles to all relationships. It is alienating, isolating and deeply disturbing. When people feel shame, the self is exposed. This makes it difficult for them to relate. Even their relationship with self is negative and they bring this negativity into relationships with others.

Many people carry a lot of shame from past painful experiences like sexual, physical, emotional, or spiritual abuse. This makes it difficult for them to establish healthy relationships with others. How many couples suffer from such past abuse situations?

Shame is a very painful emotion which we may have learned in childhood when maybe our siblings, parents or teachers shamed us frequently. So we learned to shame ourselves. But we can learn not to carry on this behaviour pattern. We have to ask ourselves: "What do I say to myself in certain situations in which I feel ashamed?" We can change the thought patterns and reduce the amount of shame considerably. We can also learn that the degree of shame in the here-and-now is contaminated and increased through shame experienced in our past life. As we work through past shame, the shame in the here-and-now will decrease.

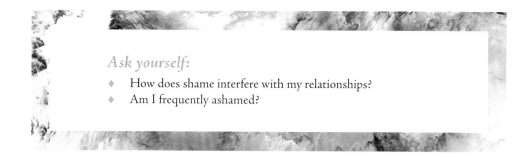

Ask yourself:

♦ How does shame interfere with my relationships?
♦ Am I frequently ashamed?

Depression

When things get too much we give up. Depression is like defeat and has become a frequent problem in our society. It is an emotional state characterised by lack of joy in life, little or no interest in work, feelings of sadness, hopelessness, lowered self-esteem, and a great deal of self-depreciation. Depressed people become slow in their thinking and actions. They have little energy and appetite and suffer from disturbed sleep.

One of my clients who suffered from depression for several years and did not want to take further medication said: "I want somebody to listen to me". In one of the sessions she said: "I am learning many things from my depression." Depression is a window to the soul. It is a mood. Like any emotion it can give us many insights into our functioning and behaviour. It has messages for us to which we need to listen and respond. It is not a matter of 'getting over it', but of accepting it and using it. Depression can be a self-imposed purge. The pain of depression can be the pain of self-actualisation. A reshuffling of values, structures, expectations and wishes may be necessary.

Anger that is not expressed outwardly can lead to depression. It seems to be all right to feel anger at life or at oneself, but the person may have learnt that it is not right to feel anger towards a person you love. The partner may say he is not angry with his wife; he is just depressed and can't work. The same person may say: "I hate to see her have to go back to work, but she'll have to support the family for a change."

Depressed people feel a decrease in self-confidence. This leads to loss of interest and withdrawal. One of the hallmarks of depression is the paralyzing sense of helplessness. Depressed people need to regain faith in themselves. They also need their family, friends and partners to care for them, to support them, to encourage them and sometimes to hold them. It is often difficult for women to ask others to care for them. This may be one of the reasons why more women than men suffer from depression.

A depressed person needs the help of others. The person who suffers from helplessness and can't move needs the listening ears and helping hand of an understanding friend.

Depression needs dealing with, we must not allow it to rule us. It is important that we look at our thought patterns and discover how we depress ourselves. As we become more aware of them, we can change these thought patterns which we may have learned in childhood. By being gloomy or of low spirits we may have attracted the attention of our parents. We may have learned this behaviour to get the attention we needed. As adults we can find healthier ways of getting the attention of others.

Depression distorts our perceptions. The greater the intensity of depression, the greater the distortion becomes. The world appears distant, uncaring and alien. When the depressed person needs understanding, love and support, friends feel barred from providing him or her with these.

People's image of God also changes when they are depressed. They see God as angry, uncaring and far away. It is hard to pray or sense anything about God. There seems to be a wall separating them from God.

Even more distorted in depressed people is their view of themselves. They lose the sense of personal worth and goodness and experience themselves as unlovable, unattractive, worthless, bad and inferior. All this makes them feel guilty. Overwhelming guilt becomes a source of deep pain.

From all of this, it follows that depression negatively affects our relationships with other people. Many cannot cope with depressed people and avoid them. They become isolated, which is the last thing they need. It is important that we learn to understand depressed people and to support them.

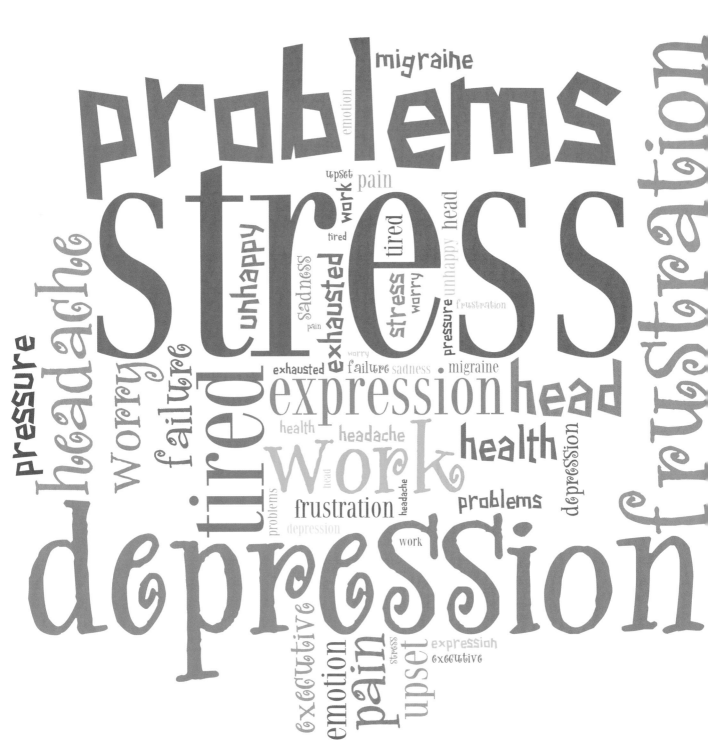

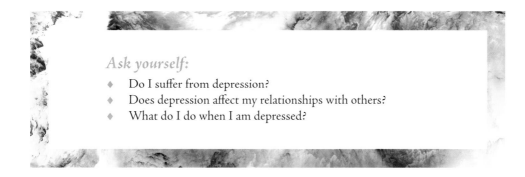

Ask yourself:

♦ Do I suffer from depression?
♦ Does depression affect my relationships with others?
♦ What do I do when I am depressed?

Stress

When people are stressed, they experience irritability, impatience, anger, depression, lack of confidence and excessive worry. Obviously all of these emotions interfere with good relationships. Other people find it difficult to be with such a person and they avoid them. It is important that we find out what stresses us. A certain amount of pressure is sometimes good for people so that they are motivated to do things, to finish a job they wanted to do. Stress is different from pressure.

When I feel stress I have an opportunity of learning to set priorities. We can ask ourselves: "What have I to do today? What can wait for tomorrow or next week or next month?" Stress may be due to many factors. It gives us an opportunity to find out more about what leads to stress and to change what can be changed. Worry, envy, jealousy, fear, anxiety, constant anger, perfectionism can all lead to stress. How we deal with our emotions may increase or decrease our stress. We may have learned a way of handling these emotional patterns in our childhood. Now, as we become aware, we can change these behaviours and be more constructive with our emotions.

We may have learned to repress our emotions or some of them. Repression uses up a lot of energy. By allowing ourselves to become aware of our emotions, and by feeling them without acting them out, we have more energy which may be used for doing the things which we need to do. This may reduce our stress.

Those who have learned to repress their anger can learn to become aware of it, to name it, own it and feel it. This will bring energy into their system. Others may have learned to act out their anger. They get angry over small things and use up a lot of energy by acting out their anger. They can learn to contain it. They may also be able to reduce the frequency of anger by changing some of their expectations which they learned as children, and some of their self-talk and perceptions. Again in this way they save energy and reduce the stress.

Stress can teach us much about our unhealthy behaviour patterns which we acquired in childhood or over the years and which can be changed so that we can live a much healthier life and prevent burnout.

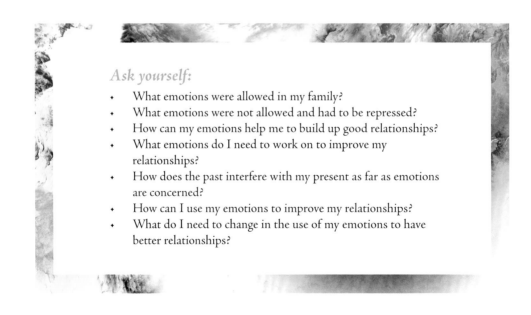

Ask yourself:

+ What emotions were allowed in my family?
+ What emotions were not allowed and had to be repressed?
+ How can my emotions help me to build up good relationships?
+ What emotions do I need to work on to improve my relationships?
+ How does the past interfere with my present as far as emotions are concerned?
+ How can I use my emotions to improve my relationships?
+ What do I need to change in the use of my emotions to have better relationships?

Conclusions

Emotions play a major part in our relationships. A joyful face can be a powerful tool to foster healthy relationships. An angry face brings fear into our relationships. Too many fears interfere with our relationships, such as fear of authority, of men, of women, of police etc. Anxiety about meeting strangers can block us from widening the range of our relationships.

Healthy guilt feelings can help us to maintain good relationships, whereas unhealthy guilt feelings may interfere with our relationships. Guilt feelings can destroy healthy relationships. People don't want to be blamed. Shyness is an obstacle in many relationships, because shy people are afraid to talk, to assert themselves and often keep silent.

Both jealousy and envy are often barriers to healthy relationships. Some people when they are hurt stop communicating with each other. Shaming people destroys relationships. The shamed person may find it extremely difficult to establish a healthy relationship with the shaming person. Shame alienates and isolates people. Depressed people often become isolated, because many people can't cope with them.

People keep away from stressed friends who are irritable.

Just as we have learned these emotional behaviour patterns, so we can learn to change them and develop behaviour patterns which foster relationships.

Chapter six

Tools for freeing ourselves from the past

Unlearning certain destructive behaviour patterns

As children we learned many things which now, having acquired new knowledge and had many new experiences as adults, we may need to update. We may have learned to keep quiet when visitors came to our family and now we still keep quiet and say very little when a visitor arrives. We may need to give ourselves permission to talk freely to visitors. This may be difficult, because we are not used to it and may feel uncomfortable because we don't know what to say. Making efforts to have a good conversation will help us to learn what to say. As we experience success, we will start to enjoy entertaining our visitors. I had to learn to do it and look forward to it now.

From various sources, we may have learned that material things are the most important factors in our lives. Later, we may feel there is more to life than material things and we may want to search for other values. In spite of all we have, we may feel worthless, inadequate and unloved and maybe confused. What we learned previously no longer resonates with our personal experience. Instead of striving just for material goods, we may decide to work towards improving our self-worth and finding deeper meaning in our lives.

My parents may have called me a 'bad boy' each time I felt angry and showed it. Now at my age I often feel bad because of what I learned in the family as a child. I now need to learn to distinguish between me as a person and my actions. Because I felt anger and sometimes shouted I was not a bad boy, although my shouting may have been unacceptable. I also need to learn to allow myself to feel the anger, without hurting others or myself. It is a challenge for me to unlearn old behaviour patterns and learn new ones which are more constructive and mature.

In some families there is much verbal, physical or drug abuse. Children may learn these behaviour patterns which cause them many problems as they grow up. As they become aware of these destructive ways in their relationships, they need to make a clear and determined choice to change them. What they have learned they can unlearn and replace with other behaviour patterns. They may need role models for that, which they did not have in the family. They may find these in TV programmes, novels, the Bible or among their friends.

Children may not learn healthy boundaries in their families. They may learn to do what they want because no one challenges their unacceptable behaviour. Their parents may have been brought up in a very strict family with many rules and little freedom. From their own negative experience they decide to give their children freedom but go to the other extreme. As these children grow up, they need to become aware that they can't just do what they want all the time. They have to change this mentality and this behaviour and acquire different habits. They have to learn boundaries, to be aware of other people. Often they will only learn them through painful negative experiences. Reading this book may help them to become aware of areas in their lives which need unlearning and they may choose to change them without having to go through such painful experiences. For example, they need to learn the importance of time-keeping. Being on time for school, work and for social engagements shows respect for other people.

Some parents want their children to be perfect and point out every mistake they make. The children learn that they cannot achieve their goals because they constantly fail. This affects their self-worth very negatively. Simultaneously they learn to criticise others when they, in turn, make the slightest mistake. This behaviour alienates them from their friends. Since it is a habit, they are not aware of what they are doing and do not understand why their friends react in the way they do. They think that their friends should be grateful for the help they are giving them to see their mistakes. People with this behaviour pattern need to unlearn this overcritical attitude and use the positive side of it constructively.

In some families children learn to delay finishing a job. They never learn to do something on time. This behaviour pattern will cause them many problems later in life where people expect them to finish a task within a given time. When people become aware that they have learned to delay things, they can decide to change this behaviour pattern realising that delays may have serious consequences.

Children may learn to blame their siblings if things go wrong. Later in life they do the same with others and they find that people avoid them and they become isolated. People do not want to be blamed for something for which they are not responsible. A person who has acquired this behaviour can unlearn it by refraining from blaming others and taking responsibility for their own words and actions.

There are many more behaviour patterns which, as we become aware of them, we may want to change or unlearn and replace with others which will help us to foster healthy relationships.

Updating our knowledge

Sometimes we just need more information about a situation or institution. The information we received as children may no longer be relevant for us as adults. This happens especially in the field of religion. God is the Being which we can neither see nor hear. But we do have Jesus who became man to show us what God is like. As children we have to use our imagination to acquire some image of God. Just as we acquire more knowledge in the various fields of science, so we also need to update our God-image. If we neglect to do that, our knowledge of God may become irrelevant to our lives or may contradict scientific insights and we may lose our faith.

Similar things apply also to the important area of bringing up children. We may have been brought up in an anti-authoritarian way with hardly any boundaries. We struggle now with this method because of the negative effects it had on us. We do not know what kind of upbringing we should give our children. We might become very strict with them, as was the case before the anti-authoritarian approach to education. This is a whole area which needs much reflection and knowledge, because we are shaping our future society.

We need to prioritise according to our essential values. There are so many things we would like to do and most likely so many books we would like to read. Deeper meaning in our lives is an essential element for our enduring happiness. Finding and fostering this is a priority in our lives. We all need solid foundations. For Christians, we have the person of Jesus in the gospels and the rest of the New Testament. Also, the new Catechism will help people to update their knowledge about the Catholic Christian faith.

Unless we constantly read new books critically on these and other topics, we may no longer be aware of new insights which humanity acquires through much research. Obviously, we have to choose what is essential for each one of us.

Ask yourself:

♦ What new knowledge and insights do I need to acquire about God?

♦ Is my God representation still the one of my childhood?

Break our transferences which interfere with our present life.

a) *What is transference?*

Transference is acting in our present adult state like we did as children. It is an unconscious process. We can become aware afterwards, as we reflect on our present behaviour, that it was well out of proportion to the present situation. We may have experienced very strong fear or anger, or both, of an authority figure who is usually gentle, caring and supportive. These feelings are triggered because the person unconsciously reminds us of some authority figure in childhood. It may be a teacher, a parent, an uncle or aunt or a neighbour.

Transference is a very common process which happens in all of us at different times. Usually when we are tired we are more prone to such processes. They may be very painful. An example from my life will illustrate this. I was in a meeting with my staff. One female member looked at me and made a comment. All of a sudden, I felt disturbed and was in pain. I could not understand what was going on. After the meeting I had time for myself and tried to analyse what had happened. This female staff member had very similar facial expressions to my aunt, of whom I was afraid as a child. My pain and confusion left me when I had gained this insight. Next day when I met this staff member she said to me: "You are afraid of me." She was right, I had been afraid of her in the meeting. Her face had triggered the transference.

b) *How to break transferences*

We need to become aware of what is going on in us. Once I became aware that my aunt's face was the trigger, I gained power. This staff member was not my aunt. She only had a similar face. I also became aware that I am no longer the little boy, but an adult with lots of experience and skills which I did not have as a child. I looked at the differences even in the face. Only what I call the 'sour look' was similar. The staff member's nose was longer, her forehead had no wrinkles, her overall face was broader. I became aware of these facial differences, and focusing on all of these differences helped me to avoid a future transference with regard to this staff member.

Usually people do not analyse such transference situations and they experience many similar painful experiences so that they find it difficult to relate to the person concerned. They are actually not relating to the present person, but to the person in their past life. In such situations they are not living in the here-and-now, but in the past. The other person may also be confused by such behaviour.

The more we can clear out our transferences, the better we will be able to live in the here-and-now and the more energy we will have in our bodies. Transferences bring a lot of tension into our lives. They take place in all kinds of situations and make it difficult to have good relationships with authority figures, friends, partners, our own children, workmates and other people. It is important to become aware of our transferences and then to dissolve them so that we can have a real relationship with these people and not a contaminated one.

c) How to detect transferences?

If our reactions to a present situation are very strong, not appropriate to the present situation, then we can be sure that it is a transference situation. Something in the here-and-now triggered this transference. It may be a physical similarity to a person in the past or the tone of voice, or what they are wearing. There are as many triggers as there are people. Very often the emotions displayed in such situations are out of proportion to the situation. People may get extremely angry or extremely frightened or feel deeply humiliated or horribly criticised.

I was at a day course in London. As we were working in pairs, my partner got very angry with me as I did with him. I felt deeply ashamed as it was discussed in the group and one person was encouraged to help us sort out our problem and become reconciled. The rest of the group were observing the procedure of reconciliation.

Although we were reconciled, I still felt the pain, shame and anger. I went for a long walk and reflected on what had happened. I realised that I had had a transference to my partner which I recognized in the intensity of my fear and anger. It was my neighbour I was angry with and afraid of and projected it on to my partner. The weight of the shame pointed to another transference. I had learned that good Christians should be examples for others. And here I was, a Christian, fighting with my partner so that we needed another person to reconcile us.

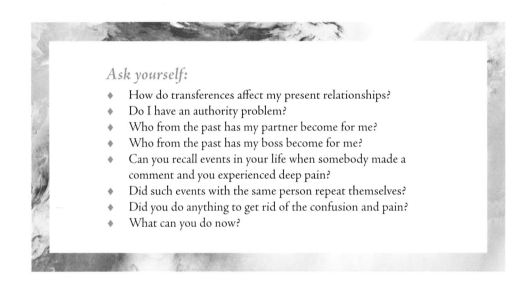

Ask yourself:

♦ How do transferences affect my present relationships?
♦ Do I have an authority problem?
♦ Who from the past has my partner become for me?
♦ Who from the past has my boss become for me?
♦ Can you recall events in your life when somebody made a comment and you experienced deep pain?
♦ Did such events with the same person repeat themselves?
♦ Did you do anything to get rid of the confusion and pain?
♦ What can you do now?

Learning to sort out conflicts as soon as they arise

Some people are afraid of conflicts because of those they experienced in the family. They will try to avoid sorting out any conflict. There is much 'unfinished business' in their life and in their present relationships. The fear of conflicts in childhood is still dominating them and they make every effort to avoid potentially conflictual situations. They need to work through their fear of conflicts, to be able to live in the here-and-now and face them in their daily life.

As we know, life is full of conflicts which need to be faced and sorted out. There are many conflicts within us. Should I talk to this person or should I avoid him or her? Should I buy this pair of shoes or should I buy that pair? Should I choose this friend or another? Should I go to the football match or the singing competition? Many interests conflict with each other and we have to choose between them. We cannot manage everything at the same time.

We may still have many childhood values and at the same time have acquired new values which we consider more appropriate for today. These two may be in conflict with each other. I value my parents, but I also value my boyfriend or girlfriend. I feel I should spend more time with my parents and at the same time I would like to spend more time with my friends. I am torn between the two. I have strong feelings of attachment to my parents and also strong feelings for my friends. When I am with my parents, I feel I should spend more time with my friends. When I am with my friends I have strong feelings to be with my parents.

Since I have not sorted out my inner conflicts, I bring these into my relationship with my parents and my friends. They feel I am not fully with them. The conflict gets worse. We all need to become aware of our inner conflicts and learn to sort them out so that we do not bring them into our relationships with other people. This would be the ideal. The reality is that we do all bring unresolved inner conflicts into our relationships with other people..

Conflicts between people are normal in human relationships. They can help us to sort out inner conflicts which we have not yet resolved. They are an opportunity for personal growth and development. I need to ask myself: "What do I do in conflict situations? Do I become afraid and run away from them or do I become aggressive and fight in such situations? Do I constantly smooth things over and never sort out any conflict? Do I constantly compromise my values when it comes to conflicts? Have I a mentality of winning any conflict? Do I go into a victim role when it comes to conflict? Am I not assertive enough to sort out conflicts?"

If we deal with conflicts constructively, we shall grow and become better people. What have we to do? We need to talk calmly to each other about the conflict situation and listen to each other, trying to find a solution to our problem which satisfies the needs of both parties. This will take some time, but it is time well spent. Both have an opportunity to become more aware of what is going on in themselves by listening attentively to the other and to their own feelings, thoughts, expectations and assumptions. Awareness may lead to changing expectations, assumptions, and thought patterns.

For example, two friends Mary and Peter have a problem with each other. Peter often feels that Mary does not love him. Mary cannot understand this, because she is so fond of him. He wants her to treat him as his mother treated him and do everything for him. Mary sees him as an adult and treats him as an adult and not as a child. She grew up fairly independently and expects the same of Peter. As they share their feelings and expectations about each other, they become aware that they differ greatly. Since they listen carefully to each other, have deep love for each other and are able to communicate well with each other, they both change their expectations and try to adjust to these in a healthy way. They know that both of them have to grow to become mature adults. Peter has to become more independent and Mary more understanding of Peter and more interdependent. Mature adulthood is an ideal, but we can grow in the direction of this ideal.

What kind of strategy do I use when a conflict arises? Do I fight? Do I withdraw? Do I negotiate? Do I compromise? It is important that we become aware how we deal with conflicts. We learned these strategies most likely in childhood and carry them on in our present life. We need to ask ourselves: "What are the consequences of the strategies I use in conflict situations for my relationships? Do I live on a surface level because I avoid facing any conflict? Do I constantly fight with my friend or partner over little things?"

How we deal with conflicts depends very much on how important our goals and our relationships are for us. If my goals are the most important things in my life, I will fight for them. If my relationships are the most important things for me, I will attend first and foremost to my relationships.

As I become aware of what I do in conflict situations, I can decide to change the strategies I learned as a child and learn new ones. I can acquire several strategies, each suitable for different conflict situations. My behaviour can become much more appropriate to the present situation. I am no longer ruled by my past life experiences. I become a freer person who can live in the here-and-now more fully.

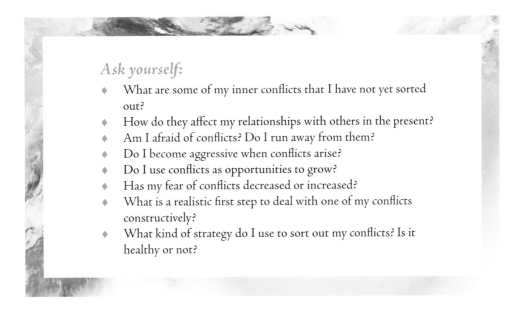

Ask yourself:

♦ What are some of my inner conflicts that I have not yet sorted out?
♦ How do they affect my relationships with others in the present?
♦ Am I afraid of conflicts? Do I run away from them?
♦ Do I become aggressive when conflicts arise?
♦ Do I use conflicts as opportunities to grow?
♦ Has my fear of conflicts decreased or increased?
♦ What is a realistic first step to deal with one of my conflicts constructively?
♦ What kind of strategy do I use to sort out my conflicts? Is it healthy or not?

Learning to forgive and, where possible, be reconciled

When we are hurt, we find it difficult to forgive. We feel fear and anger. As we brood over it, these may turn into feelings of revenge and even bitterness. We may decide to avoid the person and have nothing to do with him or her in the future.

What happens to us in this whole process? As we ruminate, we constantly hurt ourselves and generate negative feelings which may interfere with our health. Some people live in the past for decades and do not want to let go of the hurt; nourishing feelings of revenge when the occasion arises. This is not just a personal process, it can be a process that affects a whole country, tribe or class. What happened in Kosovo or Rwanda some years ago? Obviously there were deep-rooted feelings of revenge, festering maybe in the unconscious. These were ignited and led to the horrible massacre of hundreds of thousands of people.

If we find it difficult to forgive, we need to begin by learning to forgive small hurts which happen daily and increase the degree of difficulty as we acquire more skills in forgiving. First we need to be motivated to forgive. The insight that we cannot afford not to forgive because of the damage we cause ourselves, may help us. Spiritual and religious motivation can be a powerful means to help us in forgiving. For me Jesus, my model, motivated me to forgive the deepest hurts I have experienced when I reflected on his powerful words from the cross: "Father forgive them, they do not know what they are doing." (Luke 23:34)

Once we have the motivation, we need to decide that we want to forgive. We can call this intentional forgiveness. Besides this, we need to aim to forgive emotionally, which is a much longer process, because the emotions of revenge, fear and anger need to give way to understanding the person who hurt us.

We can use a chair exercise where we sit on one chair and imagine that the other person is sitting on the chair opposite us. Then we start talking to the person who hurt us. We need to express our feelings of hurt, fear and anger. Once we have done this, we change chairs. We sit on the other chair and respond as if we were the other person. The response may go like this: "I never intended to hurt you. I was very anxious and that is the reason why I said these things. I am so sorry for the pain I caused you…" This exercise can be repeated until the anger and fear are replaced by understanding the other person. Often this leads to true forgiveness.

Ask yourself:

♦ Are there people in my life whom I have not forgiven?
♦ Do I carry much resentment in my life?
♦ Am I aware of the damage to my health my unforgiveness and bitterness may be causing?
♦ Do I want to change this?
♦ Do I forgive my partner when he or she hurts me, or do I accumulate such hurts in my memory?
♦ What will be the effect of such accumulation of hurts in my memory for our future relationship?
♦ Am I ready now to begin to forgive some of these hurts and to let go of them?
♦ What motivation do I need to be able to forgive people?
♦ Do I ever pray that I may be able to forgive?
♦ Could Jesus become a model for me in forgiving?

Conclusions

Too often our past contaminates our present. Therefore we need to free our present from the past. We may have to unlearn many things which we learned as children. Some values of childhood no longer serve us as adults. We have to acquire other values and let go of previous outdated ones. We may have appreciated all the attention which we received in the family and still expect as adults, and may be disappointed that we no longer receive this attention. We have to change our expectations and strive to become more social beings.

Often we have to update the knowledge we acquired as children. We do this in many areas of our life. Some areas may get neglected; for example knowledge about God, the way we bring up children and so on.

Often transferences interfere with our present relationships. We may have experienced our boss as we experienced our father, mother or teacher as children. Usually these transferences cause us authority problems in the here-and-now. We need to break them and get rid of them.

We may never have learned to sort out conflicts. It is essential for our relationships that we learn to deal with conflicts constructively and not leave them unresolved, particularly also our inner conflicts which we might unconsciously bring into our relationships with people.

We all have to learn to forgive and where possible be reconciled. Forgiveness is a pre-condition for peace.

Chapter seven

Applying this to various types of relationships

What we discussed in former chapters, we can now apply to various types of relationships. How can we free the present from the past in romantic relationships, family relationships, in relationships at school, in friendships, in the work place and with public figures? Real-life examples will illustrate how the past affects the present and how we can free our present relationships from the negative effects of past experiences.

Family relationships

We can divide this part into romantic relationships and relationships among various members of the family

a) *Romantic relationships*

This relationship is one of the most important in human society, on which future generations depend and are built. Much support and encouragement is needed. Falling in love may be a very spontaneous event, and fostering and maturing in the romantic relationship may initially be easy, but it becomes more strenuous as the two shed their masks and show themselves as they really are. However, it is a very exciting journey, provided the two are ready to work at their relationship. It is not just a journey of discovering the uniqueness of the body but the uniqueness of the whole personality, and not just of the partner but of both. It is in intimate relationships that we find ourselves.

George, the father of a large family whom I know very well, told me how much he enjoyed the time when he fell in love with his girlfriend Grace. They just talked with each other and shared their dreams of having many children. Both came from large families.

They talked a lot about how they would bring up their children. This topic was the most common subject of their discussions. They soon found out that they had very different ideas about how to bring them up. George was used to an authoritarian approach in which the father had the last word. Grace, who had lost her mother and oldest sister as a young girl, was much more liberal and overprotective of children. Both of them had to learn to listen to each other and find a middle way.

They came from two different cultural backgrounds and had to learn a lot about their different cultures. This took much time and was not even finished when they got married. They still had to work on this matter when the daily problems with their children arrived. When George was too strict with them, Grace would intervene and he did not have the last word. She, too, learned more boundaries and discipline from him. This balance of finding the right approach went on through all their lives and with each child.

I was amazed how George changed over the years and became, in his old age, an idol for the children, whom I heard saying: "We have such a lovely father." I know fatherhood was hard work for him and he had to go through much suffering and pain.

Celebrations were frequent in their family. Christmas, Easter, All Saints Day, other feast days, birthdays, baptisms, confirmations and weddings were the many occasions they used to celebrate. They played an important part in holding the family together. Guests were always welcome and quickly made themselves at home in the family.

Commemorations are important for romantic relationships. The romance needs to continue till death. It need not involve much money but it means giving special attention to the partner. Romantic relationships are meant to build each other up, to help each other grow in love and obviously in love for self. This special attention to each other will contribute to their growth journey. The two are meant to share whatever they have, not just goods but their ideas, values, ideals, life experiences, frustrations, joys and worries. In all of this they have many opportunities to support each other and become enriched through their intimate relationship.

Flowers played a major part in any celebration, because his wife was very fond of them and later had many in and round the house. George would never forget her birthday and would always bring her some flowers, which she appreciated. Grace, in return, prepared delicious meals for him, especially on his birthday and feast days. She was also expert in decorating beautiful candles for such occasions.

Each person is unique. Each one has talents which may be hidden and which need to be discovered in the relationship, so that both get a chance to enrich their lives. Each person also has weaknesses and worries and needs to be supported by the partner. Sometimes the partner may have similar weaknesses and worries and it may be difficult to support each other in these areas. They may need outside help.

Many aspects have changed and are changing in romantic relationships in our time. However, today personal work on the romantic relationship is even more essential than in the past as the understanding of roles and expectations has changed. Each partner needs to refrain from blaming the other and take responsibility for their part in the relationship. Only by doing so will they make progress in their journey together. This will involve a lot of work, even suffering and pain. However, the outcome of such hard work is inner freedom, peace and joy.

Christian values, with Christ as a model, helped George and Grace to accept this often painful journey. The crucifix in the sitting room reminded them constantly of what Jesus had suffered, and brought much stability into the family. Even when George could no longer talk because of a stroke, he would go in front of the crucifix to find consolation. When he was unconscious for seven weeks and I visited him in Grace's presence she said: "Don't die, I will look after you." He lived nine more years and Grace did look after him lovingly and well.

It would be foolish to expect romantic relationships to be without struggles and crises. They are part of such a journey and are tools for the personal growth of the two partners. Often the most difficult situations are occasions for us to gain tremendous insights and knowledge. Marriage is a great chance to mature.

b) *Relationships among the members of a family*

Family members need a lot of support to be able to make the best of what family life is meant to be. Many parents have never had healthy experiences in their own families. Their father or mother may have been an alcoholic, a drug addict, a gambler, a racist or a depressive person. Obviously, these factors will influence family life and the development of the children.

Most parents bring into their families what they have learned in their own families. In a patriarchal family they may have learned that the father is the head of the family and everybody follows his orders. In a matriarchal family they may have learned the mother is the boss of the family and everybody has to do what she says.

Parents' cultural and religious backgrounds will also influence their family life. A couple came to me for counselling. He was English and she was Irish. They had separated. He lived in a flat and she lived in the house. As they shared their experiences of family life, it became clear that their cultural backgrounds played a major role in the problems they encountered.

For example, when I had a session with the husband alone, he said to me: "I get very angry when my wife tells me that I do not love my daughters. I do love them." He did not, however, express his love for them in the way his wife expected him to. He was brought up with a 'stiff upper lip' background and was not so emotionally expressive. Once several of these differences were clarified and both of them learned more about the two different cultures, to appreciate them and change what they found useful to change, they came together again and led a very happy and fulfilling family life. The cultural differences became assets.

Preparation for marriage would need to be much longer and deeper. The two would need to look at their prejudices and work through them. They would also need to become aware of their destructive behaviour patterns and start to change them. Our efforts need to go into improving family relationships so that the family becomes the place where children learn healthy behaviour patterns and attitudes. Healthy families are a solid foundation for Church and state. Any investment in improving families and their relationships will pay off in the long run. Pope Francis ratified this by convening a Synod on family life.

Often transferences interfere with relationships in the family. Becoming aware of, and understanding, their own transferences helps spouses and partners to relate to each other in an adult way. They can ask themselves: "What expectations have I of my partner? Can my partner fulfil these expectations? Are my expectations realistic? If my spouse does not fulfil my expectations, how do I react to him or her? Do I feel put down because he did not bring me flowers for Valentine's Day? Do I feel rejected because she forgot my birthday? Are these emotions strong? Where do all these things come from? Are these expectations I had of my father or mother? Do I project my father or mother on to my partner? Whom does the husband transfer on to the wife? Whom does the wife transfer on to the husband?"

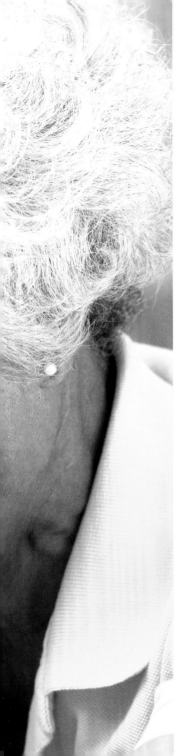

Understanding our own transferences will help us to relate to our partner in a more adult way. A wife may expect her husband to take the role of her father whom she adored and on whom she depended. How does she see a marital relationship? She may need a clear understanding of what a marital relationship is and then adjust her expectations for her husband. She knows that a marital relationship is a relationship between two adults which has been formalised by the marital contract. The assumption is that both adults are mature and have reached a stage in their development which we can call interdependent. They are no longer dependent on their parents or parent-substitutes like they were as children. There are many kinds of dependencies such as financial, emotional and physical dependencies. As nobody achieves complete mature interdependence, there are always elements of transference in marital relationships. They are unconscious and can interfere with the adult relationships.

Interdependence means that the two persons rely on each other for their basic needs to be met. The social structures of the family are interdependent. Families depend on the state, the school, the police, the priest, the doctor the dentist and so on. The state and the Church depend on the parents to fulfil the basic duties of bringing up their children. They have to see that they go to school. If they are believers, they take them to religious services. Parents have a responsibility to look after the physical, psychological and spiritual wellbeing of their children.

Some parents may have never had the experience of being looked after in all three areas: physical, psychological and spiritual. They may need to learn the basics in any or all of these areas to provide what is needed for their children.

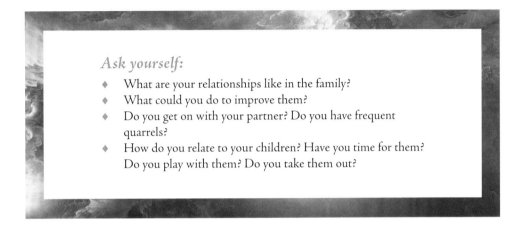

Relationships in school

A pupil frequently gets anxious and can't perform well when the teacher introduces new topics. He does not want to go to school. The teacher is generally perceived as a very gentle person, willing to help any pupil who asks. Francis, however, is afraid to ask but does not know why. The parents discuss this situation with the teacher who finds it difficult to understand what is going on in his relationship with their son. The more the teacher tries to talk to him, the more he seems to withdraw. Finally the school counsellor is called in to see Francis.

The boy takes to him and shares what is going on for him in his relationship with his teacher. The counsellor is trained in dealing with transferences and soon finds out that the voice of the teacher reminds him of his father. He is afraid of his father, particularly when he comes home drunk and withdraws to his bedroom.

The counsellor helps him to see the differences between his father and the teacher. Francis replies to the counsellor who asks him what the differences are between his father and the teacher: "They have a similar voice. Both are tall." As the counsellor helps him the relationship between Francis and his teacher gradually improves. The teacher has black hair, whereas his father has brown hair. The father has brown eyes, whereas the teacher has blue eyes. The teacher wears a suit, whereas the father wears casual clothes. The teacher is kind, the father is very strict. The teacher asks questions, the father demands things from him. The teacher listens whereas the father always talks and does not give Francis an opportunity to talk.

As he works through his transferences onto the teacher, he gets to like him and his studies improve. Now he is very happy to go to school and has started performing well.

Relationships with friends

To have good friends makes life much easier. Without friends many people would be lonely and would not get the support they need. Some people cannot establish friendships. They are too self-centred and no relationship will last. They may be too shy and do not dare to talk to people or get engaged in a deeper discussion. Often they are not even aware of this fact because they blame their so-called friend when things go wrong. They may not be aware of their shyness or their self-centredness because they are so used to it. It has become a habit.

When I did research for my doctoral thesis about religious and moral attitudes of young people, I was surprised at some of the answers: "When I have nobody to go to, I always have Jesus to whom I can talk and with whom I can share anything that worries me." This shows us the importance of religion and particularly of a deep relationship with God. Such a relationship can carry us through the most difficult situations in our life. Therefore it is important that we either start such a relationship with God or deepen it. It is a great investment for our survival and happiness.

It is normal for difficulties to arise in any friendship and this means also in our relationship with God. There are many reasons for this. Often we bring unfinished business from our past life into our present relationships. This may be repressed anger which we could not air when we were small and so it may be triggered in the present. One of my clients said to me: "I cannot stand a dominant God and I have problems with my head teacher." As he explored his relationships, he became aware that he had a very domineering mother.

Claire and Sonia have been friends for many years. They support each other as much as they can. However, Claire gets annoyed when Sonia tells her what to do. Sonia, in turn, cannot stand it when Claire orders her to do certain things. Although they are friends they keep at a certain distance from each other. Both of them had mothers who were demanding and told them constantly what to do. Although they did not like this aspect of their mothers, they ended up learning the same disliked behaviour patterns.

As soon as one of them displays this pattern, the other goes into a transference with her mother and experiences all the 'put-downs' of childhood. Obviously, neither of them is aware of what is going on in the unconscious. This makes it difficult for both of them to become more intimate with one another.

As they reflect more on this deeper dynamic of their behaviour, they will be able to distance themselves more from their mother transferences and their relationship will improve.

However, Claire has a strong sense of privacy and needs a lot of time for herself which is often experienced as a rejection by Sonia. Sonia wants more togetherness, compensating for her lack of it in childhood, where she did not experience it much with her sister and mother. Claire had plenty of togetherness with her younger sister and has no need for it which comes across to Sonia as not being interested in her.

Ask yourself:
- What are your relationships like with your friends?
- Do you support each other? Is it one-sided?
- Do you frequently lose friends? If so, why?

Relationships in the workplace

Anything that can be done to improve relationships in our workplaces is welcome for everybody. There are two main areas which need tackling: one is power struggles and the other is authority problems. Both have to do with relationships. For good relationships we need to have good communication and be able to manage our emotions constructively.

John is a very hard worker in a factory. His boss is very pleased with him. He is reliable, honest and committed. Sometimes, however, his boss forgets to inform him about certain matters which he should know, because he has ten people working under him. In such situations John gets extremely angry with his boss, although the lack of information does not cause too much inconvenience. It takes him days until his relationship with the boss is again on good terms. Both he and his boss cannot understand why he reacts in such a way.

When he shared it with me, I helped him to go back to his childhood and find out where this came from. He discovered that as a child, when one of his teachers did not like him, he did not do so well as his brothers and sisters so he learned to find out things from his father which his peers did not know. He then appeared to have more knowledge than his peers who could be proud of their academic achievements. This gave him a sense of superiority compared to his brothers and sisters.

As he became increasingly aware that such knowledge in the present situation was no longer so important for his self-esteem, he became much calmer with his boss if he forgot to tell him something which he should have known in his position. John would still mention it to Peter, his boss, but both of them might have a good laugh instead of being unduly upset over it.

Their good relationship became more stable and both saved more energy for their work. Peter also found out that sometimes he would unconsciously withhold information from others as he had done as a child which gave him a sense of power. This awareness helped Peter to share information; he had power via his position in the factory. He no longer needed to withhold information to feel powerful.

Their relationship improved considerably. Both of them felt that they were true friends who had established an intimate relationship by sharing their childhood experiences. They have been working together for over thirty years and even during the economic crisis their factory was performing very well. They are able to maintain a good atmosphere among workers who are willing to work hard. Everybody is willing to cooperate since both of them are now role models for the workforce in the factory.

Ask yourself:
♦ How is your relationship with your boss?
♦ Do you avoid him or her?
♦ Are you afraid of him or her?

A teacher called Robert was very supportive of students, particularly those who struggled with their academic achievements. He would do anything to help them pass their exams. Once he went too far in preparing them. He gave them topics to study that appeared in exams, which got him into trouble.

He found it very difficult if one of his students failed the exams. Some of his colleagues considered him proud when all his students succeeded. However, he seemed otherwise to be an exceedingly humble person. Nobody fully understood him; neither did he understand himself.

At a public exam, out of 'concern' for his students, he leaked the questions for the exam. They all passed, whereas many other students failed. There was a public inquiry. He was found out and the principal of the college did not know what to do. Robert seemed to be such a good, involved and committed teacher. He himself was very upset at what he had done. He could not understand why he had let himself down in this way. He was an honest and upright man. Why would he do such a thing?

They agreed that he would see a therapist. After four sessions, it became very clear that an unconscious motivation was at work. He himself struggled as a student. His teacher was very hard on him and shamed him each time he failed his exams. He was determined to become a teacher himself and do the opposite, namely to support the students as much as he could. The defence mechanism of 'reaction formation' was at work in this situation. He went to the other extreme of 'helping' his students. Robert's unconscious motivation carried him away even to cheat in exams, which he himself could not understand.

Relationships with public figures

Marion, an African lady of twenty, was raped in London but was afraid to report it to the police. In Africa as a child Marion was told: "Keep away from the police or you will be imprisoned." With this fear she came to England. When friends encouraged her to report the rape, she pleaded with them not to go to the police, as she was afraid of them.

Finally a friend whom she trusted reassured her that the police in England were different from the police in Africa, so she dared to approach them accompanied by her friend. The friend explained to the police how fearful she was and why. They received her in a very friendly way and she responded by telling them the whole story of being raped.

As she was sharing her story she remembered that she had been sexually abused by her uncle who looked after her when her parents had died of AIDS. She was so afraid of men that she did not trust any man.

However, the encounter with the police woman who helped her to express herself and later with a policeman who was very gentle with her, helped her to be healed of her strong fear of police and men. She no longer avoided them and learned to relate to them in a healthy way. Marion was aware that when she was raped by the man she could not resist because she froze.

Slowly she was able to develop healthy relationships with both men and the police. She felt much freer in herself and could enjoy life again. Before, she was dominated by a constant fear and did not know what it was all about.

Relationship with God

This is our most basic relationship because we are creatures and He is our Creator. This relationship is the foundation of all other relationships and needs to be acknowledged as such. Without a true understanding of the fundamental relationship, on what do we build our relationships? Is it on sand? Is that the reason why society seems no longer to be able to cope with the many problems which come its way?

We need to foster our relationship with God through prayer, meditation and the celebration of the sacraments. Every relationship needs nurturing. Often we neglect to do this and gradually our relationships die because they are no longer meaningful for us.

In particular our relationship with God is in need of tender nurturing, since God is the Being we cannot see. We have constantly to update this relationship as we grow and mature. It is a relationship of belief and trust. The material for this relationship comes very much from our experience of mother, father and other people with whom we have close contact. Therefore it is in constant need of being purified and updated.

People who do not update their God-representation may lose their faith, because their knowledge about God is no longer in line with other knowledge they have acquired. They may still have the concept of God which they learned as children. I have listened to a programme where an atheist shared why she no longer believes in God. The God she described was a "childhood" God. Her understanding of God had remained at that level.

Ask yourself:

♦ Have I any relationship with God? Would I like to develop such a relationship? How would I profit by having a deep relationship with God?

♦ Do I struggle in my relationships with people?

♦ Am I aware of the cause of my struggles?

♦ If not, observe what goes wrong in your relationships: Do your emotions interfere with them? Do you lack the skills of good communication? Are you too shy? Are you not assertive enough?

♦ Do I really want to improve my relationships? Try to find reasons why you truly desire to do something about them.

Conclusions

Applying the insights of this book to all our relationships will create an atmosphere around us which leads to healing, peace, reconciliation, happiness and inner freedom. Romantic relationships will lay a solid foundation for the relationships in the family. The members of the family, particularly our children, will grow up in an atmosphere which will be nurturing, supportive and encouraging, instilling constant hope in them.

In schools where these insights are practised, this process will continue to help in preparing our next generation for the difficult tasks in our society, supported by healthy friendships and good relationships in the workplace. Public life, economy and the whole of society will profit through improved relationships, in which people no longer suffer constantly from the contamination of past experiences. Society and the whole of life will be involved in a process of constant healing, maturing, supporting and growing. No area of life will be excluded from this. The whole of society and the Churches will become part of this process. All of this will happen in small steps, but steps which will be worthwhile and fruitful for all people.

Chapter eight

Conclusion: Into the future with hope

Various ways and means to go into the future with hope

Most people dream of a happy future. Some work for such a future, others wait for it to happen. You have already started the work by reading and applying the insights of this book to yourself. It is just a matter of continuing this journey and experiencing the benefits of your labour. When we work hard, we want to get something out of it.

Hope is a virtue which we can learn from the life of Jesus and the disciples. What happened when Jesus died on the cross? The disciples' lives were shattered. They had hoped that he would be the one who would establish his kingdom on earth. Now he was dead. Like Jesus' body their hope was buried for three days. They could not see into the future. They were disheartened and disappointed.

Then hope entered into their lives again, as they heard that he had appeared to some of them, and later to many of them. Since the resurrection of our Lord there is always hope for all of us. Therefore, whatever our past might have been, we want to go with hope into the future. We free ourselves from the past: from certain expectations, aspirations, behaviour patterns and many more things. We want to learn from our previous mistakes and then move on and not get stuck in the past. We need to make good the effects of our mistakes, as far as we can, and then let them go. We may still want to work on changing some of our behaviours.

So far this book may have helped us to become aware of many aspects of our behaviour that we would like to change. Partly we may have succeeded in doing so. In other areas we may need to find other tools and get more help from experts in those areas. We may have acquired the insight that this process of healing needs to continue for the rest of our lives. We may even be excited and adventurous in persevering in this search for healing, and becoming a more mature and integrated person. We may even see it as part of our mission and vocation to deepen God's kingdom in us and become more Christ-like by becoming a more loving and forgiving person.

Relationships are daily food or poison or both for most of us. Perfect relationships are a dream and are only found in the relationships of the Blessed Trinity. Our relationships need much exciting work. How and where do we go from here? With hope we go into the future and make efforts to improve our relationships on all levels. We have many means and skills at our disposal. We may still need to develop more skills, like being assertive. What we cannot achieve ourselves, provided we do what we can, we ask Higher Wisdom to lead us and are open to her inspirations.

There are so many levels of relationships. A very important one is how we relate to ourselves. Again, there are so many aspects of relating to ourselves. Do I accept my past experiences, my nationality, my culture, my parents and siblings, my childhood, my adolescence, my schooling? Do I accept every part of my body or are there certain parts which I hate, for example, my gender, my height, my ears, my nose, my legs, the shape of my body? How do I relate to the environment? Do I act out my anger by destroying things around me such as furniture, crockery, etc? Am I afraid to look at the core of my being where I may encounter God, as one of my clients was terrified to do? How are my relationships with others?

Some people may continually have problems in their relationships because they experience constant stress. Besides following the guidelines mentioned in all chapters, it may help to reduce the tension by receiving regular massage, aromatherapy, doing relaxation exercises or going for a walk on a regular basis. Because we build up stress in our daily dealings, we need to find a way to relax so that we do not live in unrelenting stress. Ongoing stress wears us out and interferes with our relationships.

If you find that your emotions, like anxiety, anger, fear or guilt feelings, cause you many problems, body work therapy can help you to get rid of the stored up and imprisoned emotions in your body. You can experience much relief and freedom. It also relaxes the body and will help you to improve your relationships.

People may need counselling or therapy to work through certain traumas in their past life. None of us has escaped one form or other of trauma in our past lives; many are no longer aware of those traumas, which they have repressed, and which still affect their behaviour in the here-and-now. Whatever our age, we can work towards being able to live more fully in the here-and-now and not be too contaminated by our past experiences. As we work through these, even the most negative experiences can become an asset. Once we have dealt with the negative effects of our traumas, the strength and insights which we gained, as survivors of traumas, still remain and help us in many situations.

All of us can profit from using spiritual resources. We can tap into the deeper levels of our being and use methods of meditation and prayer which are suited to our uniqueness. For me, my model is Jesus Christ. He has influenced my whole life. I have learned so much from him and I am still learning much more every day, as I meditate on his life and teaching. Through meditation on the suffering of Christ, I have learned to see value and meaning in my personal suffering. When I had endocarditis and was in hospital, I always had Rublev's icon in front of me, which reminded me of the Blessed Trinity. Before my open heart surgery I was calm and relaxed. My faith gave me the strength, courage and hope which I needed to go peacefully into the operating theatre.

You may decide to become a member of a Church, if you do not yet belong to one. You may feel that you need the fellowship of a community to support you.

Spiritual direction is a powerful means of developing our spirituality. Many people in our time have a longing for deep spirituality which is the cement of our society, our families and relationships. It is highly useful for young people to develop their spirituality long before they involve themselves in deeper partnerships. Without a deeper meaning in life, partnerships can easily deteriorate and remain on a surface level.

Spirituality is more than reading the Bible, praying and meditating. It is a healthy way of living. Christian spirituality means living a life of love as Jesus lived it. He gave his life for us to redeem us and to restore us to friendship with his Father. We can all increase our ability to love ourselves, others and God. We can all become better lovers as long as we live. Loving more and better will improve society, our neighbourhood, our families, our friendships, our work place, our political sphere and our economic systems. We can all contribute to an emerging better world.

Money and other material goods alone are no guarantee of a happy life in the future. We need more permanent values which Christianity and other religions can provide for us. We need to face the fact that we are mortal, so that we can live life fully. Life passes more quickly than we realise. It is important for us to ask ourselves: "What comes after this life?" It is also important for us to be able to face death. It is all around us. The four seasons in nature remind us every year of dying and rising. If we avoid facing death and live as if we were in this world forever, we avoid looking at the deepest aspects of our being. Deep in all of us is a desire for immortality, a life after death. To face it without faith may be too anxiety-provoking.

We are in a dilemma. Do we want to continue not sorting it out? Or do we want to lead a deeper life, a fuller life, a life in which everything somehow makes sense, even pain, suffering and death? We have to study the life of Jesus who went through all of these dreadful sufferings. However, they were not the end of his life. What followed after his death, namely the resurrection, gives hope to all of us. Christians believe that he died for us so that we may live with him for ever, because just as he rose from the dead, so shall we rise and live a life with God. This is what gives meaning to our present life.

This is the greatest hope a person can have. Millions of people have lived in that hope and many even gave their life because of their belief in Christ. So strong was their hope, that they had the courage to die for Him rather than give up their faith in Him.

My hope and prayer for you, is that you find a deeper meaning in your life so that you can lead a happier and fuller life without extreme fears and anxieties but much joy, peace and fulfilment. We only live once in this world. Let us make the best of it in preparation for the fullness of life to come.

Ask yourself:

- ◆ How do I see my life? Is my main focus on material things?
- ◆ How can I deal with daily stress in a better way? What support do I need for reducing my stress?
- ◆ What do I need to do to reduce my anxiety?
- ◆ How can I improve my overall wellbeing? Could I build a daily walk into my routine?
- ◆ How can I deal with my guilt feelings which burden me? Do I need to change my expectations of myself and be more realistic about what I can do? Do I need to be superman or superwoman?
- ◆ How can I improve my spiritual life? Could I ask a good spiritual director to help me in this process? How would this support my happiness in daily life?
- ◆ Who is Christ for me? If I deepened my relationship with him, how would this change my life?
- ◆ How do I need to change my self-talk in order to lead a happier life?
- ◆ Is my inner dialogue full of 'shoulds' and 'oughts'? How can I change that dialogue?

What is my hierarchy of values?

I may have acquired a hierarchy of values which was satisfying for me in the first half of my life. Experiencing mid-life crisis, of which I may not be aware, I feel that nothing makes sense any more. I feel dissatisfied with my life. I may be disillusioned because I expected more of life. I may even feel depressed. It may be necessary to look at my values and discover why I am no longer happy with the way I lead my life.

If we want a happier future, we need to look at our hierarchy of values. What is really important in my life? What do I treasure most? Our values affect our relationships. If material things are what I value most, I will sacrifice relationships when they interfere with acquiring material goods. If relationships are my highest value, when it comes to certain conflict situations between relationships and material things, I will opt for relationships.

When I was at a funeral and I looked down at the coffin in the grave, the thought came to me: "What would you like people to say about you when you have died?" The answer came: "You brought love into people's lives". This is what I would like people to be able say about me. It is important that we clarify our real deep values and do not keep on living according to some of our immature childhood values.

The desire for spiritual values is becoming stronger in our society, especially in the last few decades. Many people look for spiritual values. They try to find them in all kinds of things. Some of them turn out not to be true spiritual values at all. I can only share those values with you which have ruled my life. I found them in my Christian faith which I treasure more than anything else. For many people throughout the world, Pope Francis exemplifies values like simplicity, love for the poor, acceptance of our sinfulness and the loving mercy of God.

If our society as a whole came to accept these values wholeheartedly, what changes would take place? How would these changes affect our economic system? What kind of life could the majority of people live? How would our churches have to change? How would all these changes affect family life and relationships? Would we all become people who can relate out of love for each other?

I met a mother of three children from Slovenia. She told me that she tried to imitate the simple lifestyle of Pope Francis in her family. She talks with her children and husband about how simply the Pope lives. Together they have adopted this simple lifestyle which affects the whole of their family life and relationships. They are inspired daily by the way Pope Francis tries to live as Jesus wants us to live. If Christian values become the basis of our relationships, our family lives will become more stable.

Although we had little money after the Second World War, and sometimes we had to count the slices of bread we ate, we were happy. We enjoyed the toys which we ourselves made and gave to each other as Christmas presents. We tried to live our Christian faith and prayed together daily. I have many lovely memories of the very simple life we led.

Ask yourself:

♦ What are my values? Write down the ten most important values for your life. Look at them with a critical eye and develop a healthier hierarchy of values for your future life.

♦ What can I learn from Pope Francis? How could that affect my life and my relationships?

We need to become experts in sorting out conflicts, forgiving, and being reconciled where possible

Conflicts are daily food or daily poison in our relationships. Some conflicts we can prevent, however, there are many conflicts which we cannot. We need to acquire an ability to deal with conflicts constructively. Conflicts can be a tremendous source for personal growth and development when we tackle them in the right way.

It is important that we prevent as many conflicts as we can, because to sort them out is time- and energy-consuming. It is better to try and prevent them. If I am very busy one day and do not want to be interrupted, I can tell people in the morning that I need time and ask them kindly not to interrupt me. In this way I can prevent possible conflicts from arising. People will respect my need and let me get on with my work.

By providing people with the necessary information, I can prevent misunderstandings which are often the cause of conflicts. For leaders, it is essential that they provide those entrusted to them with the necessary information to carry out their work. That is the reason why we need clear job descriptions. People know then what we expect of them. As leaders, it is also important that we know what those entrusted to us expect of us. Without clarifying our expectations many conflicts may arise.

If we learn to sort out simple conflicts, we will become more expert in sorting out more complicated ones. Running away from conflict is not a solution. It is very understandable why some people don't want to face conflict. Their experience of conflicts in childhood may have been very negative. But as adults they have many more skills and can learn to face small conflicts first, then increase the degree of tackling more difficult ones.

We can also acquire more skills which we need to sort out conflicts constructively. We can learn to listen actively, to be empathic, to be immediate, to be more assertive, to confront caringly, to check that we have heard correctly, not get emotionally entangled, to be compassionate, and so on. All of these skills will help us in sorting out conflicts in order to live a more peaceful and fruitful life.

Sorting out conflicts will help us to deepen our relationships in family life, among friends and in the workplace. As we sort out our conflicts with others, we get to know them and ourselves better. Self-awareness will encourage us to change certain behaviour patterns which we acquired in childhood and which are no longer appropriate for us as adults. As long as we live, we can become better people, more loving in the way we relate with ourselves, others and God. Thus, a hope-filled future awaits us when we work on our relationships.

Ask yourself:

- How do I deal with conflicts? Do I run away from them? Do I constantly provoke them? Do I try to sort them out?
- How can I use my conflicts for personal growth and development?
- How will sorting out my conflicts improve my relationships?
- When it comes to conflicts, do I still act like a child?
- How assertive am I in conflict situations?
- How can hope help me in my future life?
- Do I build my future life on hope and trust or on mistrust and doubt?
- How can my hope help my family, my partner, my neighbourhood?

Conclusions

We all need hope as we go into our future. Hope will support us as we encounter obstacles on our journey. The Christian faith will show us the meaning of the pain and suffering which will come our way, knowing that these are not the last things. They lead us to joy, freedom and the resurrection as they did with Jesus. On this journey we have so many opportunities to practise and grow in love.

As shown above, we have also many means of support on our exciting journey which goes through death to resurrection. Even our conflicts become means for this inner journey provided we use them constructively and learn from them. All the time we are called to forgive and, where possible, to be reconciled. This will lead to deepening our relationships as we continue to strip them of the contamination of our past experiences.

Our whole journey becomes one of healing, of constant excitement, of experiencing, deeper than the pain, inner peace and freedom. All of this will contribute to a better world with more peace and freedom. Let us continue with hope the journey we have begun by reading this book. The author wishes you a liberating and fruitful journey and prays for each one of you.